THE
Paper·Pieced
HOME

QUILTING A HOUSEHOLD ONE BLOCK AT A TIME

Penny Layman

INTERWEAVE
interweave.com

Acknowledgments

A big thank-you to *Joelle*, *Linda*, *Kerry*, *Glynis*, and *Tara*. Your friendship, support, and love throughout this process have meant so much to me!

Special thanks to my editors, *Michelle* and *Allison*. You two are amazing women, and I am so thankful and honored to have you in my life!

Thank you also to *Laurie Wisbrun* for believing in my craft way back in the day and to *Rob Blackard* for allowing me to use your shoe illustration to create the men's fancy shoe pattern. Also to *Robert Kaufman* fabrics for supplying me with a few solids from their Kona line.

To my husband, *Lenny*, thank you for your input and encouragement and for taking a part in my "fabric stuff," even though it's not your thing. Your perspective has kept me grounded, and always will. Thank you for having my back. I love you!

Lastly, thank you *Aunt Joan*. You have loved and helped me immensely through difficult times and I am so blessed to have you.

This book is dedicated to my parents, *Leon and Sharon*. I love you and miss you both.

Editors Michelle Bredeson and Katrina Loving
Technical Editor Rebecca Kemp Brent
Associate Art Director Julia Boyles
Designer Brass Bobbin Creative LLC
Illustrator Missy Shepler
Photographer Joe Hancock
Production Designer Katherine Jackson

© 2014 Penny Layman
Photography © Joe Hancock
Illustrations © 2014 Interweave
All rights reserved.

 Interweave
A division of F+W Media, Inc.
4868 Innovation Drive
Fort Collins, CO 80525
interweave.com

Manufactured in China by
RR Donnelley Shenzhen.

Library of Congress
Cataloging-in-Publication Data
Layman, Penny.
The paper-pieced home : quilting a household one block at a time / Penny Layman.
pages cm.
Includes index.
1. Patchwork—Patterns. 2. Quilting—Patterns. I. Title. II. Title: Quilting a household one block at a time.
TT835.L393 2015
746.46—dc23
2014016301
ISBN 978-1-62033-597-0 (pbk)
ISBN 978-1-62033-599-4 (PDF)

10 9 8 7 6 5 4 3 2 1

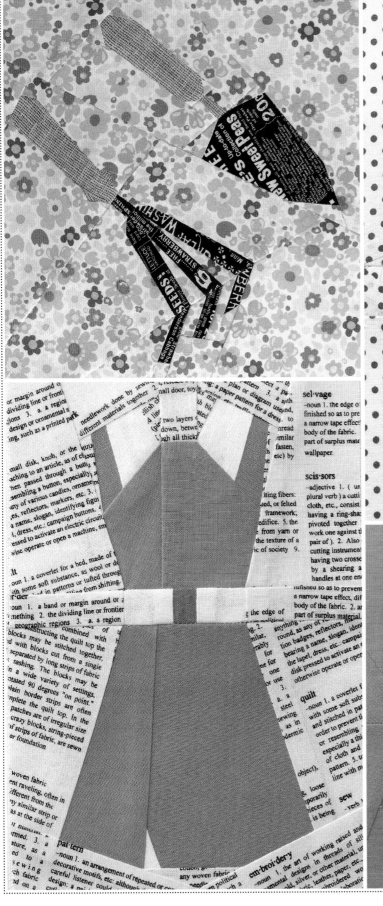

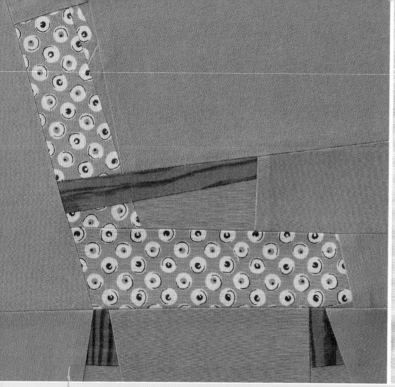

Contents

Paper Piecing Is Fun!

My love for paper piecing was born out of a desire to learn how to paper piece different objects around my house that I cherish.

I started out trying to improvisationally piece a few objects like a chair and a cupboard with stacks of fabric on it. Although the end results were charming and one of a kind, I realized I wanted to get a more precise result that could be recreated. I began researching techniques and stumbled upon paper piecing. After many hours of looking online, I found little to no support for learning how to do it, so I contacted my friend Ayumi Takahashi and asked her if she would be interested in starting an online bee that focused on original paper-piecing designs. We came up with the name "Ringo Pie." We chose this name because we both love food, and because the Japanese are brilliant at piecing intricate blocks. *Ringo* means "apple" in Japanese, and we all know what pie means.

We got busy and put together a list of people to ask and they all said yes, which was a pleasant surprise. I am so thankful for all the women in the Ringo Pie bee. Their talent has pushed my desire to achieve new levels in paper piecing!

Paper piecing is also called foundation piecing. For those of you who have never tried the technique, foundation piecing is just that: piecing a block onto a foundation layer.

The foundation layer can be fabric or paper. If you piece onto a fabric layer, the base layer of fabric will be a part of the finished piece. If you piece onto paper, the paper will be removed once the block is completed. In this book, we will use paper as the foundation layer.

Because you're sewing onto a foundation layer of paper, paper piecing allows for creating blocks that have tiny areas of detail that would be impossible to sew accurately with just a template. This is one reason I love paper piecing. The detail can be amazingly complex and once you have the concept down, the piecing part is as easy as sewing a straight line.

I liken paper piecing to putting together a jigsaw puzzle. It can be time consuming, but the process and the end result give me a strong sense of accomplishment. Because of this, paper piecing is indeed fun!

I have always had a strong sense of "no nonsense" and tend to create things that are useful. Paper piecing allows me to put a little fun and whimsy into the useful home projects I make. In this book, you will find forty block designs, representing everyday things in your home that you may see and use, as well as ten projects that use those blocks.

Happy piecing!

—Penny

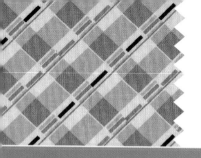

CHAPTER 1

Getting Started

Hi, friend! I'm so glad you decided to start at the beginning to get a good foundation and understanding before you start your paper-piecing journey with my book. In this first chapter, you will find invaluable information about what supplies you will need, the basic paper-piecing steps, and tips on choosing the right fabrics for your blocks and projects. A good understanding of these three topics will help to streamline the process as you begin your journey.

Basic Supplies

Through tons of experience and trial and error, I've finally come to the conclusion that having the right tools makes a big difference in paper piecing. This section describes all the supplies I use for paper piecing. Most of the tools I've listed are probably found in your sewing room already, but there might be a few others you will want to purchase.

PRINTED FOUNDATION PATTERN

The first thing you will need is your printed foundation pattern. On the accompanying CD, you'll find foundation patterns for all of the blocks shown in this book. When you

tip

When you print a pattern, be sure to choose a page setup to print at 100 percent.

print a pattern, be sure to choose a page setup to print at 100 percent. Once you print the pattern, double check the printed block size with a ruler so you don't end up with a block that is too large or too smallt.

Keep in mind that your paper foundation pattern is the mirror image of what your block will look like. In other words, your pattern is the reverse of your finished block.

There are several brands and types of foundation-piecing paper available. Some are very thin, making the removal process very quick and easy. Some are made of vellum, which makes fussy cutting easier since you can see through the vellum to fussy cut the precise area of fabric you desire.

To cut down on expense because of the sheer amount of paper I go through, I tend to use plain printer paper, but I highly recommend you try some of the specialty papers until you get the hang of the process.

SCISSORS

I use my craft scissors to cut paper foundation patterns because paper quickly dulls scissors and I don't want to ruin my fabric shears. I use a small pair of fabric scissors or a rotary cutter to trim seam allowances.

FABRIC

Choosing fabric for a pattern is time consuming but so satisfying! When I've found the right fabrics for a project I usually get a "settled" feeling in my gut. I try not to start sewing a project until I have that feeling, because if I rush the decision I usually end up having to redo the project. See Choosing Fabric (page 16) for more tips on selecting fabric for your blocks. I typically use quilting cotton when I paper piece, but if I come across a scrap of special fabric (for example a piece of chenille or home décor material) that will add a little something special to a block, I'm happy to use it!

Note: The block patterns in this book include suggested sizes for scrap fabrics used to make the block. It's always good to have a little extra on hand for generous cutting, fussy cutting, and potential redos.

Super-Size It

Some of the blocks in this book are larger than a standard-size piece of paper. For blocks larger than 8" × 10½" (20.5 × 26.5 cm), the patterns are divided into multiple pieces. You will need to print them on several pages and tape them together. Don't worry about sewing over the tape; your machine will be fine.

SEWING MACHINE AND ACCESSORIES

I do all of my paper piecing on a sewing machine. The type of machine is not important. I use a microtex 80 (also called a sharp) needle when I piece. It has a very slim point and is very accurate. Also, I find my ¼" (6 mm) presser foot with a guide is very useful as I paper piece. I don't pay attention to the guide as I'm piecing each section, but I do use it as I sew sections together for accurate seams. Another option is an open-toe presser foot that allows complete visibility as you sew along the printed lines, or you can use your all-purpose presser foot.

THREAD

For paper piecing, I use a thread that is strong and thin. Of course we all want our thread to be strong, but I also want it thin so it doesn't take up a lot of room in the seam allowance. A 50-weight thread works well, such as Aurifil 50 weight (wt).

My must-have paper-piecing supplies.

SEAM ROLLER

A seam roller is one of those tools I wouldn't have found out about if it weren't for my paper-piecing addiction. Now I use it for all my sewing. A seam roller presses without distorting the fabric and makes the paper-piecing process go much faster because you can keep the seam roller right next to your machine and it allows you to avoid ironing after each addition of fabric. Don't confuse the fabric seam roller with a wallpaper seam roller. A fabric seam roller is 1" (2.5 cm) wide and has a curved surface and beveled edge.

SEAM RIPPER

Because you're working backward and seemingly upside down with paper piecing, it's easy to sew the fabric on incorrectly the first time by putting the raw edge on the wrong side of the sewing line, by using too small a piece of fabric, or by sewing the right side of the fabric to the wrong side of the paper. Because of my paper-piecing addiction, my seam ripper has become my best friend for ripping out stitching mistakes. I use a thin, sharp seam ripper that looks similar to a surgical blade. The blade is removable so when it gets dull, it can be replaced easily.

TWEEZERS

A nice, thin, pointy pair of tweezers gets a lot of use in my sewing studio. It comes in handy to pluck out those pesky threads left behind by removing seams and to also grab bits of paper off the back of your block once you're done piecing.

RULER, ROTARY CUTTER, CUTTING MAT, AND FORK PINS

Other must-have tools are a 1" × 12" (2.5 × 30.5 cm) acrylic ruler with a ¼" (6 mm) seam mark, a small- to medium-size rotary cutter, and fork pins. I use the rotary cutter with a cutting mat for cutting the initial pieces of fabric, sometimes for trimming seam allowances as I paper piece, and for trimming around each section. Fork pins are amazing tools when you are sewing sections together and need to match up a seam in one section to a seam in another section. I like them better than regular pins because of the two tines. You place a tine on either side of the matched seam when sewing sections together so there is no shifting. This allows for more precise seam matching.

FABRIC GLUE STICK

I use my Karisma fabric glue stick almost every time I paper piece. Instead of pinning my initial fabric to the paper pattern, I glue it. The fabric glue stick won't distort the fabric like pinning does and it won't leave a residue. It provides a light-enough hold that you can remove your fabric and reglue it if your fabric placement is off.

IRON AND STARCH

I have yet to find the perfect iron, so kudos to you if you have! The features that are important to me in an iron are that it gets red hot and the sole glides over the fabric. Because of all the problems I've had with irons beginning to leak over time, I tend to use a dry iron and use spray starch generously. Use whatever brand of spray starch you like. Because I go through so much spray starch, I usually make my own using 16 oz. water, 1½ teaspoons cornstarch, and a few drops of essential oil in a spray bottle. This mixture will have to be shaken to mix it each time before you use it.

Basic Steps

The process of paper piecing may seem counterintuitive and backward at first. My hope is that as you learn the technique and begin to understand how paper piecing works, you will become more comfortable with the process.

READING YOUR PATTERN

A paper-piecing pattern, or foundation, is the basis for all paper-pieced blocks in this book. (The patterns for the blocks are included on the accompanying CD.) As you begin to paper piece, it's very important to know how to use and read your pattern.

You will be sewing fabrics to the unprinted side of the printed pattern, with the fabric right side down and the printed pattern right side up (wrong sides together). Because of this, your finished block will be the reverse of the printed paper pattern.

tip

The patterns in this book have the individual areas colored in for you, but if you're using a pattern that is not colored in, be sure to color in each area or mark the area with the color of fabric you will use before you start so you don't get confused and sew the wrong fabric to an area. Colored pencils work well for this.

Here is a list of the different lines and notations you will find on the patterns and what they mean:

Numbers
Each pattern area is labeled with a number. You'll piece the areas of each section in numerical order, from 1 through the highest number.

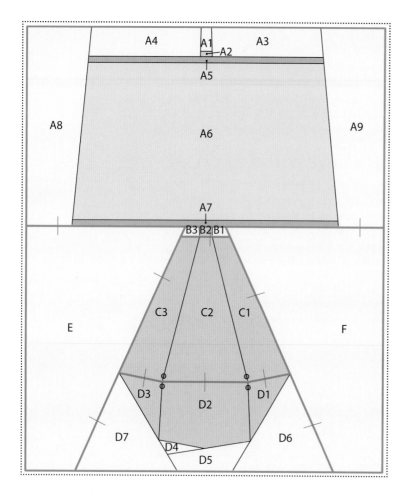

Letters

Sections are indicated by letters. If you have a pattern with no letters, the pattern is all one section and can be sewn in one piece. If your pattern has letters, you will cut the pattern into sections along the blue lines, piece each section according to the numbers, and then sew the sections together.

Lines

In the included paper-piecing patterns, you'll find two kinds of lines: thin, black lines for sewing and bolder, blue cutting lines between sections.

Tick Marks

When a pattern has more than one section, it's helpful to have tick marks on the cutting lines to aid in positioning the sections as you sew them back together. Tick marks are indicated by short red lines that cross the blue cutting lines.

Green Dots

The final mark you will need to be aware of is a green dot, which indicates a Y-seam (see Y-seams on page 23). There are three patterns in the book that require a Y-seam: the Sleeveless Dress (page 58), the Bathing Suit (page 57), and the Lamp (page 76). When you see a green dot near the end of a sewing line, do not sew past the end of the printed sewing line near the dot.

PAPER PIECING STEP BY STEP

Whether you are paper piecing a simple block or an intricate one, these instructions are the basics you will use over and over again. I've provided a simple single-section block to help you understand how the basic paper-piecing process works.

❶ **Print and cut out the block pattern.**
(The pattern for the sample block is on the accompanying CD.) Roughly cut out the pattern close to the outer block lines (**fig. 1**; see Tip #1). (If the pattern you're using has sections, cut directly down the middle of any blue cutting lines; see Piecing a Block with Multiple Sections on page 16.) Keep in mind that the printed side of the paper pattern will be on the back side of your finished sewn block.

❷ **Cut fabrics for each area.**
Precutting the fabrics for each area will keep you from having to stop sewing to cut the next piece of fabric. When you cut the fabric, keep in mind that not only does the fabric need to cover the visible area, it must include at least ¼" (6 mm) of seam allowance on each edge. Fabrics for areas along the outer edges of the block must extend at least ¼" (6 mm) past the edge of the paper pattern;

this is the block seam allowance. In this book, the instructions for each block indicate the amount of each fabric you'll need for the block (see Tip #2). *Note: It can be very frustrating to find out after you've sewn the fabric down and flipped the fabric open that the piece is just shy of covering the area or isn't big enough to allow for a seam allowance. To avoid the frustration, cut the pieces for each area much larger in each dimension than the area printed on the paper foundation.*

❸ **Position the first piece of fabric.**
Place the first piece of fabric with its wrong side against the unprinted side of the paper foundation, making sure the fabric extends at least ¼" (6 mm) past all edges of area 1. You can check the placement by holding the pattern up to a light source. Use the glue stick to hold the fabric in place **(fig. 2)**.

❹ **Position the second piece of fabric.**
Place the second piece of fabric, which will cover area 2, on the first fabric with right sides together. Position the raw edge of the second fabric, which will become your seam allowance, at least ¼" (6 mm) into area 2 **(fig. 3;** see Tip #3).

❺ **Sew the first and second fabrics together.**
Holding the second piece of fabric in place, flip everything over so that the printed side of the paper pattern is facing up and sew on the line between areas 1 and 2 **(fig. 4)**. Adjust your machine's stitch length to 1.7–1.8 mm (15 stitches per inch) before you begin sewing. If your sewing line begins or ends within the block (rather than at the edges), backstitch at the beginning or end of the seam line to lock the stitches in place.

❻ **Trim the seam.**
Flip the block back over to the fabric side and trim the seam allowances to about ¼" (6 mm), using a small pair of fabric scissors or a rotary cutter **(fig. 5)**. Be careful to cut only the fabrics; do not cut the paper foundation.

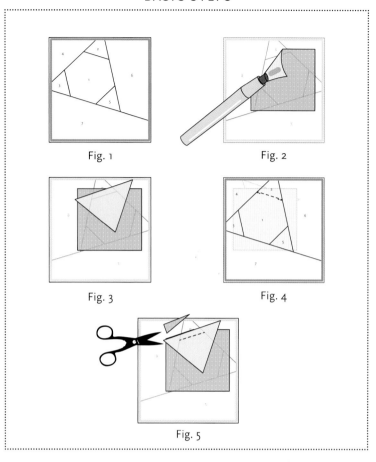

Fig. 1   Fig. 2

Fig. 3   Fig. 4

Fig. 5

tips

1 Many paper piecers leave ¼" (6 mm) of paper around the entire paper pattern, but I never do. This way, as you sew the sections together, you won't be sewing the paper seam allowance into the seams, which makes removal of the paper at the end a lot easier.

2 Once the fabric pieces are cut, stack them with the piece for area 1 on the top of the stack and the piece for the last area on the bottom of the stack. This will allow you to pull the top piece off the stack and quickly sew it to the next area.

3 Hold the pattern, with the first and second fabrics in position, up to a light so you can see whether the second fabric raw edge is positioned at least ¼" (6mm) over the sewing line.

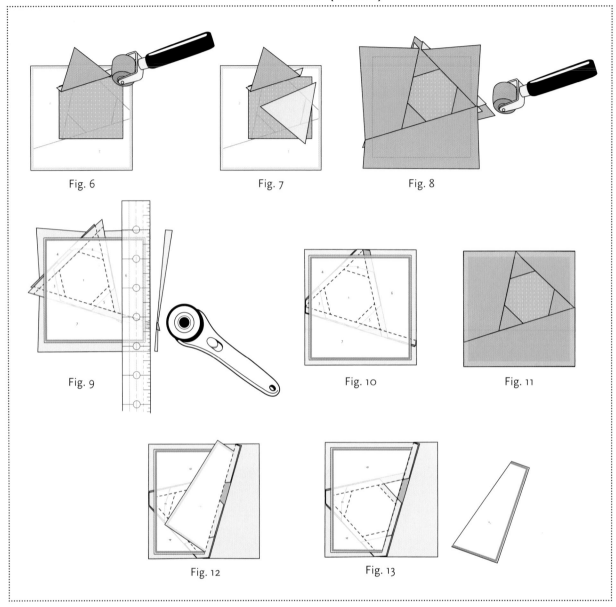

Fig. 6

Fig. 7

Fig. 8

Fig. 9

Fig. 10

Fig. 11

Fig. 12

Fig. 13

Note: Before trimming seam allowances, always double check that you are cutting the fabric on the correct side of the seam line.

⑦ Press the seam line flat.

Flip open the piece of fabric you just sewed onto the block to cover the second area. From the right side (fabric side) of the block, press the fabric open with your fingers and the seam roller to press the fabric flat and the seam line open **(fig. 6)**. Take care to open the fabric completely to avoid creating a little pocket along the seam and puckering that will keep later seam lines from matching correctly.

⑧ Position the next piece of fabric.

Place the third piece of fabric on the other two, right sides together. Remember to position the raw edge of the new fabric at least 1/4" (6 mm) into area 3 **(fig. 7)**.

⑨ Sew the second and third fabrics together.

Flip the paper pattern over and sew the second and third fabrics together on the sewing line between areas 1 and 3, following the same instructions as in Step 5 (see Tip #1).

⑩ Trim the seam.

Repeat Step 6 to trim the seam you just sewed. Once again, make sure you're trimming the correct side of the seam.

⑪ Press the seam line flat.

Follow Step 7 to press the seam you just sewed flat.

⑫ Finish sewing the block.

Repeat steps 8–11 for the rest of the areas, positioning fabric, sewing, trimming the seam, and rolling the seam open until each area of the block is pieced (**fig. 8**; see Tip #2).

⑬ Press fabric side of block with spray starch.

I like to starch the block (or section) once it is completely sewn to stabilize the fabric so I don't stretch the block as I pull the paper off the back.

⑭ Trim the block.

Use your ruler and rotary cutter to trim the fabric to ¼" (6 mm) past the paper pattern edges (or section edges if your block has more than one section; **figs. 9–11**).

⑮ Remove the paper foundation from the block.

Remove the paper in reverse sewing order by folding the paper back over the seam line, running your finger over the fold to crease it (**fig. 12**), and pulling the paper off as if you are pulling a check out of a checkbook (**fig. 13**). The close perforations of the needle made by the short stitch length will make this easier. The last area of paper you will remove will be the paper in the number one position; you may have to pinch the center of it to remove it if it doesn't release easily.

The finished sample block.

tips

1 As you sew your fabrics onto the pattern in numerical order, you will be sewing on the line between the new fabric and an area or areas with a lower number. In other words, the area you are currently adding fabric to will always be a larger number than the area(s) on the other side of the sewing line. Referring to the sample block, when you sew the third piece of fabric onto the block, you will be sewing on the line between areas 1 and 3. Then, when you sew the fourth fabric piece onto the block, you will be sewing on the entire line between area 4 and areas 1, 2, and 3.

2 When a sewing line begins and/or ends on the outside edge of the block, make sure to extend the seam line at least ¼" (6 mm) beyond the edges of the paper pattern as you sew.

Pressing Issues

Here are a few things to keep in mind while pressing:

When you press a seam open on the back of the block, the fabrics on either side of the seam will have a flat appearance from the front of the block. Also, when you run your hand over the front of the work, it will have a smooth feel.

When you press a seam to the side, the fabric that the seam is pressed toward will stand out a bit more and the fabric you press the seam away from will recede. You will also be able to feel this "stair-step" effect when you run your hand over the front of the work.

Since the pressing direction of paper-piecing seams is already determined by the numbering of the areas (the seam will always be pressed toward the area with the larger number as you add fabric), the only time you will have to consider how to press a seam is when the pattern has more than one section.

BASIC STEPS (CONT.)

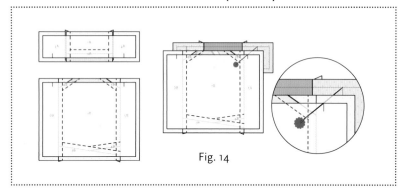

Fig. 14

PIECING A BLOCK WITH MULTIPLE SECTIONS

Piecing a block that has more than one section adds a couple of steps to your process. The biggest difference is that, in addition to cutting around the paper pattern edges, you will also cut the pattern apart on the blue cutting lines to separate the sections. Then you will follow steps 2–14 above for each section. Before the paper foundations are removed, sew the sections together in the order shown in your pattern.

When sewing the sections together, lay the sections right sides together and put a pin straight through the fabric from back to front where the tick mark meets the edge of the paper pattern. Align the tick mark on the adjoining section by piercing it with the pin from front to back; hold the pin perpendicular to the block surface so it passes straight through the fabric layers **(fig. 14)**. Hold the sections together and pin normally through the fabric layers, then remove the perpendicular pins. Sew the sections together with a ¼" (6 mm) seam and press the seam (open or to the side, whichever is indicated in your pattern).

Choosing Fabric

The fabrics you choose for your blocks will either enhance or detract from the design. Here are some tips about different types of fabrics to help you decide, before you start sewing, whether the fabrics you want to use will work for your block.

Note: Unless otherwise stated, the fabric yardages in this book are based on 45" (114.5 cm)-wide fabric with at least 42" (106.5 cm) of useable width. A fat quarter is a piece of fabric that measures 18" × 22" (45.5 × 56 cm); a fat eighth measures 9" × 22" (23 × 56 cm).

CONTRAST

According to Wikipedia, contrast is "the difference in luminance and/or color that makes an object (or its representation in an image or display) distinguishable." Understanding the concept of contrast will help you immensely as you choose fabrics for your blocks. In other words, choose fabrics for your block that will make the focal object distinguishable from the background.

Keep in mind that although you may choose fabric colors that are completely different, if the contrast between the two colors isn't high enough, the block image may appear muddled to the viewer. This can happen when the values (lightness/darkness) of the two colors are too close.

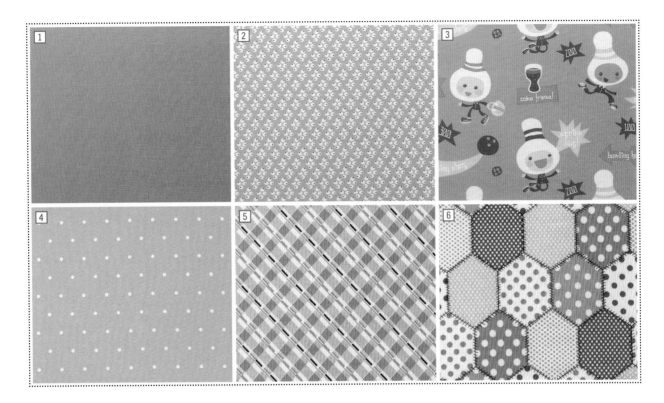

One way to check the contrast between fabrics is to take a photo of the fabrics next to each other and filter the photo to black and white. If the fabrics are about the same shade of gray, then the contrast between the two fabrics is not great.

SOLIDS 1

As much as I love prints, there's just something about using solid fabrics that really appeals to me. I think it's the clean graphic nature they lend to designs, which gives you an image that can't be mistaken.

TYPES OF PRINTS

Small-Scale Prints 2

Limited use of small-scale prints can add a lot of character to your block without being overpowering. If the print is closely spaced, it can be very useful for backgrounds or for smaller pieced areas. Be careful when mixing too many small-scale prints in the same block, however; this can make your block look kind of crazy!

Large-Scale Prints 3

These prints tend to work best for larger areas (think several inches) of a block pattern and for fussy cutting (see page 17). If you use them in smaller areas, the block will have a random look and will be nondescript.

Polka Dots 4

Polka dots can range in size from Swiss pin-sized dots to large circles. They can be random or set in a straight row or on the bias. However they're arranged, I love them! Closely spaced ¼" (6 mm) or smaller dots are very effective in small areas of a pattern as well as larger areas. If I use small dots for a block background, I do like to fussy cut the larger areas so the dots are aligned as much as possible. However if the background area is small, it doesn't make much visual difference, so I don't fussy cut.

I rarely use prints with large polka dots in paper-pieced designs because they lose their effectiveness when cut into smaller pieces.

Geometric Prints 5

Geometric prints like stripes, plaids, and checks are great for adding a strong graphic element to your blocks. However if the areas you use them in aren't fussy cut so they all flow in the same direction, they can give a really wild and random look to your block; I sometimes do it deliberately when I'm after that sort of look. The only time this type of print won't make things look a little wild is when used in only one area of the block.

Multicolored Prints 6

Prints with several colors can be very effective if used in a large, single area or the background of your block. If I use a fabric with many colors, I always pair it with a solid (or fabric that reads solid) to tone it down.

tip

If you're unsure whether your fabrics enhance the block design or detract from it, ask someone. I am constantly holding blocks up to my husband and asking him, "What is this?" If he can tell me right away what the block design is, I know I've done a pretty good job of picking fabrics.

BLOCK EXAMPLES

Now let's go through some sample blocks and really evaluate them one at a time to give you a better idea of what works and what doesn't. I've chosen the same jar block for each example to keep the focus on the fabric choices. (A pattern for the jar block is included on the CD.)

Jar 1

For the most part, I like this block. I like the fussy cutting for the lid, and the random, larger-scale print with lots of different colors works well for the jar. The only problem I see with this block is that although the lid is white and the background is yellow, there just isn't enough contrast between the two.

Jar 2

With this block, the only thing I like is the large-scale print for the jar. The background print is too large for the size of the background areas, and the white in the background dots "bleeds" into the jar and makes it hard to read the jar edges. Because the background print is too large, the top edges of the jar are muddled, and the solid green lid doesn't have enough contrast with the blue background. The quickest fix for this block is to swap the background fabric with a solid or solid-reading fabric that contrasts clearly with the lid and jar fabrics.

Jar 3

The two things this block has going for it are contrast and the jar fabric. Although I do like the fussy-cut words on the lid, can you see the white print at the bottom of the lid fabric? It muddies the edges. Also, the angles of the plaid background fabric are all over the place.

Jar 4

Jar 4 is a classic case of too many colors and too many prints. The contrast is pretty good; however, the combination of the jar fabric and the background fabric is a bit much. If either the jar or background fabric were a solid, this block would be perfect.

Helpful Hints

Here are some tips to help you as you make the blocks and projects in this book.

All seam allowances are ¼" (6 mm) unless otherwise specified.

Sometimes you will need to remove a seam because you've sewn the fabric onto the paper incorrectly. Try to keep the paper intact as you remove the stitches, but if the paper starts to tear because of the perforations from the stitching, it's not a problem. Just put a piece of transparent tape over that part of the paper pattern to hold it together.

Use a larger piece of fabric than you think you will need for each area. This will help to reduce the amount of time you have to spend with your seam ripper, ensuring that the fabric covers the intended area once you flip it into place after sewing.

Keep your seam roller, small cutting mat, and scissors next to your sewing machine. That way, as you are paper piecing, you won't have to keep getting up to cut and press each seam after it's sewn.

Jar 5

I like this block as is. The contrast is good, and the jar and lid lines are clear. The jar fabric is an excellent use of a solid piece of fussy-cut fabric, creating the suggestion of a label on the jar.

Jar 6

This block makes good use of a large-scale fabric for the jar, a fussy-cut directional stripe for the lid, and a solid fabric for the background. I can see the block design right away and know it's a jar with a lid. The contrast among all three parts—lid, jar, and background—is good. I see nothing I would improve on with this block.

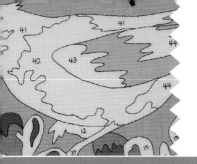

CHAPTER 2

Beyond the Basics

Now that we've covered the very basics of paper piecing, let's build on what you've learned and talk about a few more-advanced techniques that will enhance your blocks. In this chapter you will learn how to fussy cut fabric to fit into specific areas of your blocks, how to sew Y-seams in applicable patterns in this book, and a few embellishing techniques to make the blocks and projects your own.

Special Supplies

Although they're not necessary for basic paper piecing, adding details like embroidery or appliqué to enhance your blocks will require a few extra supplies.

FREEZER PAPER

Freezer paper comes in handy when I want to create a template of an area to fussy cut (see page 21). I also use it for appliqué patterns (see page 26) and on occasion for a Y-seam (page 23). You can find freezer paper in rolls or in sheets. I prefer to use the sheets because they are already cut to printer size, which cuts down on preparatory work.

TRANSFER PAPER AND EMBOSSING STYLUS

If I'm planning to embroider a block (see page 24), I use Saral wax free transfer paper to copy the design onto the block after it's been pieced. I prefer Saral paper because it can be brushed or erased away. I use an embossing stylus to trace the design.

BUBBLE JET SET 2000 AND BUBBLE JET SET RINSE

Printing on fabric with your computer and printer is a great way to add a little variety to your blocks and projects (see page 27). The Bubble Jet Set 2000 combo will first prep your fabric for the ink, and then set it for permanence.

LIQUID GLUE

A liquid glue that is fabric safe and water-soluble aids in attaching binding (see page 29) and adding appliqué. A tiny applicator tip makes it easier to apply the glue precisely. The brand I use is Tombow.

STAMPS AND INK

A few small rubber stamps and ink pads that appeal to your taste are great to keep handy for those special times when a block needs a bit of stamping to make it just right. See Rubber Stamping on page 26 for more information on which types of ink work best.

EMBROIDERY SUPPLIES

Adding embroidery to a block can add so much to the design. In addition to transfer paper and a stylus, you'll need six-strand embroidery floss (I use Cosmo floss), an embroidery needle, and, if you choose, a hoop.

Fussy Cutting

Often when I'm contemplating a pattern, I have a specific area of fabric in mind to go in a specific area of a design. In that case, I need to do what's called fussy cutting. This is easiest if the fabric I'm fussy cutting goes

A few additional supplies can help take your blocks to the next level.

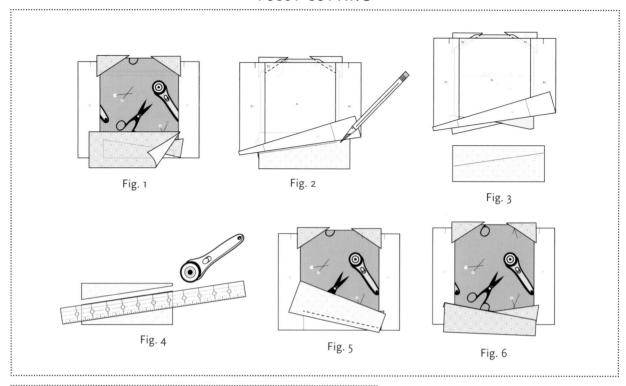

Fig. 1

Fig. 2

Fig. 3

Fig. 4

Fig. 5

Fig. 6

in the first area of a section because I can just hold the paper pattern up to the light with the fabric layered on the blank side of the pattern to be sure the print position is correct.

If I'm fussy cutting area 2, 3, or 4, etc., in which the sewing lines of the pattern might be angled, it can be very difficult to get the fabric positioned just as I would want it without a bit of help. In this case, one option is to print an extra pattern onto freezer paper and cut out the area in question. Iron the freezer-paper section to the wrong side of the fabric so that it frames the print correctly, then trim the fabric ¼" (6 mm) past the edge of the freezer paper on all sides. When it's time to sew that piece onto the block, align the corresponding edge of the freezer paper with the sewing line

I fussy cut the fabric for the wheels of the Popper Push Toy (page 112) to get the pattern to line up just right.

you'll be using (remember that the fabrics are sewn onto the blank side of the paper) and sew. You will have the perfectly sized piece of fabric at the perfect angle to achieve the results you were envisioning. Remove the freezer paper from the fabric before continuing.

The following instructions outline a faster, but slightly less precise, placement technique which is especially good for adding directional fabrics on a slanted sewing line. In the example, I'm trying to get the polka dots to align straight across the bottom of the block.

1 Position the fabric right side up on the un-printed side of the paper foundation, covering the appropriate area **(fig. 1)**.

2 Turn the pattern over, holding the fabric in place and fold the paper foundation along the sewing line. Lightly trace along the fold onto the wrong side of the fabric **(figs. 2 and 3)**.

3 Trim ¼" (6 mm) above the traced pencil line **(fig. 4)**.

4 Position the prepared fabric on the paper foundation, aligning the pencil line you drew in Step 2 with the sewing line. Hold the whole thing up to the light to better view the pattern sewing line if you need to.

5 Carefully flip the unit over, holding the fabric in place, and sew along the sewing line. Flip the unit back over **(fig. 5)**.

6 Trim and then press the seam **(fig. 6)** and you will see your fabric direction (in this case, the polka dots) lines up pretty darn well!

Y-Seams

Before we start talking about Y-seams, take a deep breath and say out loud, "I can do this!"

Y-seams (inset seams) are really pretty simple. Basically, a Y-seam is a seam that has an angle in it. And that's no problem, I say!

The Lamp block (page 76) features Y-seams in the base.

When I sew Y-seams, I always start sewing at the junction point. If I end up with extra fabric, it's on the outer edge (instead of in the middle of the block where it can bubble up) and I can just trim it off. Hallelujah!

On the patterns, Y-seams are indicated with green dots. The patterns in this book that use Y-seams are the Bathing Suit (page 57), the Lamp (page 76), and the Sleeveless Dress (page 58).

Here's how you do it.

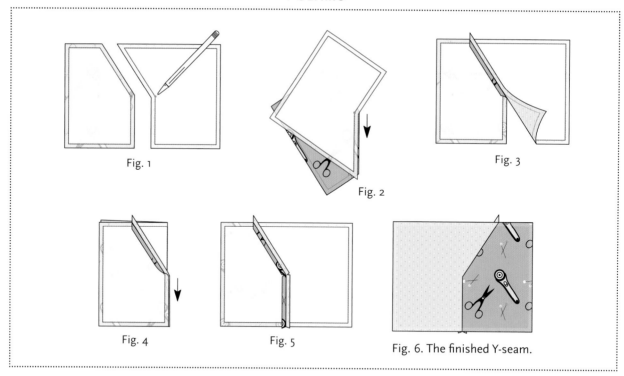

Fig. 1

Fig. 2

Fig. 3

Fig. 4

Fig. 5

Fig. 6. The finished Y-seam.

1 Use a water-soluble pen to mark the convex point (the apex) and the concave side of the junction point (**fig. 1**).

2 With the fabric right sides together, align the two dots and one pair of raw edges that will be sewn together (**fig. 2**).

3 Sew the seam together, starting with backstitching at the center dot and sewing to the raw edges of the fabrics (**fig. 3**).

4 Align the remaining unsewn raw edges (**fig. 4**).

5 Once again, start sewing at the center dot, backstitching at the dot and sewing to the raw edge of the fabrics. Clip the seam allowances at the point and press the seam allowances open (**figs. 5 and 6**). That's really all there is to it!

Embellishments

A little bit of embellishment can take your block to the next level. Although I tend to use embellishment sparingly, I do use the following techniques on occasion.

EMBROIDERY

A tiny embroidered detail can add that extra-special touch and take your block from good to great. There are many, many embroidery stitches you can use. The ones I use most often are the backstitch, running stitch, and satin stitch. The embroidery designs used in the blocks are included on the block patterns on the CD. Where necessary, reversed patterns are provided. Embroidery diagrams for the projects are printed on pages 132 and 133.

Follow these steps to transfer embroidery designs to your block:

1 Piece your block.

2 Print a copy of the block with the embroidery design onto printer paper.

3 Layer the assembled block, right side up; transfer paper, chalky side down; and the embroidery design, right side up. Make sure the embroidery design is correctly situated on the block.

4 Trace the design with an embossing tool.

Embroidery and Appliqué Stitches

Running Stitch

Working from right to left, bring the needle up and insert at 1, ⅛" to ¼" (3 to 6 mm) from the starting point. Bring the needle back up at 2 and repeat.

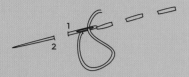

Satin Stitch

Working from left to right, bring the needle up at 1, insert at 2, and bring back up at 3. Repeat until you have filled the desired shape.

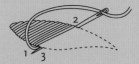

Backstitch

Working from right to left, bring the needle up at 1 and insert behind the starting point at 2. Bring the needle up at 3. Repeat by inserting at 1 and bringing the needle up at a point that is a stitch length beyond 3.

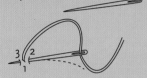

Blind Stitch

Take a small stitch in the background fabric at 1, then take the next stitch about ⅛" (3 mm) along in the appliqué fold at 2, creating a diagonal stitch; repeat until the seam is finished.

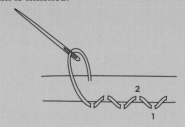

5 Lift the transfer paper and design to see if there are any areas of the design that need to be touched up; if so, use a fabric pencil for this.

6 Embroider over the traced lines using the stitch indicated in the instructions, referring to the illustrations above as necessary. Use fewer strands (2 or 3) of floss for more delicate lines and more strands for thicker lines.

A touch of embroidery, as in the shoelace for the Women's Fancy Shoe (page 60), can really dress up a block.

APPLIQUÉ

To add dimension and/or curved accents to your block, a little appliqué goes a long way.

Here are the steps:

1 Where necessary, reversed copies of block patterns with appliqué templates are included on the CD. Print a copy of the block pattern with the appliqué design onto freezer paper, shiny side up.

2 Cut out the appliqué motifs, making sure the edges are smooth. If there are jagged edges in the freezer paper template, your appliqué will have jagged edges.

3 Iron the freezer paper template, shiny side down, onto the wrong side of the fabric **(fig. 1)**.

4 Cut the fabric, leaving ⅛" (3 mm) seam allowance around the freezer paper template, and clip any curves **(fig. 2)**.

5 Using spray starch and a small craft iron, press the fabric seam allowances to the back of the freezer paper bit by bit, and then carefully remove the freezer paper **(figs. 3 and 4)**.

6 Use tiny drops of fabric glue around the pressed edges of the design to glue the appliqué onto the block fabric.

7 Hand stitch the appliqué piece to the block using an appliqué stitch or blind stitch (see the sidebar on page 25 for more on the blind stitch).

(see the sidebar on page 25 for more on the blind stitch)

RUBBER STAMPING

Another way to add personality to your blocks or projects is to stamp on the fabric. If you are going to stamp a portion of a block, here are some things to consider.

Use a permanent fabric ink, such as VersaCraft. The ink is permanent once it's set with an iron.

I've also experimented with pigment ink pads. Pigment ink pads have very saturated color and can readily be found in stamping supply stores. However, because pigment inks are

tip
If you are unsure how to do an appliqué stitch, you'll find a number of YouTube tutorials you can view.

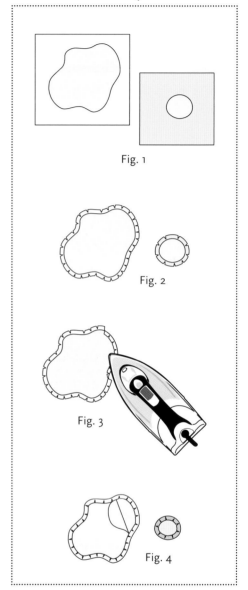

Fig. 1

Fig. 2

Fig. 3

Fig. 4

tip
To reduce the likelihood of ruining your finished project or block, always stamp on your fabric before it's sewn into your block or project.

not permanent, do not use them on any project that will be washed.

Stamp your image/words on the fabric before it is pieced into the block. Once you get a good stamped image, follow the steps for fussy cutting (page 21) to add this fabric to your block.

PRINTING WITH YOUR COMPUTER

If you'd like to add larger or different words or images to your blocks or projects than you have stamps for, you can print them onto your fabric. (The His and Hers Shoe Keepers project [on page 64] incorporates words that are printed on fabric, and the printable words are included on the accompanying CD.) The steps are a bit time consuming, but they're well worth it. To use your printer to print on fabric, follow these steps.

❶ Pretreat your fabric with Bubble Jet Set 2000 according to manufacturer's instructions.

❷ Allow the fabric to dry.

❸ Iron the fabric onto freezer paper that is sized to pass through your printer, and trim the fabric so it's the same size as the paper.

❹ Print the image or words on the fabric side of the freezer paper with your printer.

❺ Allow the ink to dry for at least 30 minutes.

❻ Remove the fabric from the freezer paper.

❼ Treat the fabric with Bubble Jet Set rinse and allow it to dry.

I printed the labels for the His and Hers Shoe Keepers (page 64) directly on the fabric.

The Clawfoot Bath Mat (page 84) could easily become a welcome mat or play mat by swapping the bathtub with another block.

Make It Yours

Altering and Substituting Blocks

I love mixing things up and doing my own thing as I'm sewing, and it's not often that I follow a pattern to the letter. Here are a few things you can do to modify blocks to make them fit into different projects or to make them more "you."

SHRINK OR ENLARGE THE BLOCK DIMENSIONS

One way you can quickly change a block is by resizing it. In most cases, you will be able to do this in your printer settings by changing the printing percentage for the image. If your printer program doesn't have this setting, you can use photo-editing software to change the size. Alternatively, you can print your block at normal size, scan your printed block into the computer, and use the printer settings to print it out at a different size or take the printout to a copy center for resizing.

So let's say you have a 6" (15 cm) square block, but you need a 3" (7.5 cm) block. When you are in the print screen, reduce the pattern to 50 percent and you will get a 3" block.

The same thing applies if you need a larger block than what is offered. If you have a 9" (23 cm) block pattern and need a 12" (30.5 cm) block, you can increase the pattern to 133.4 percent (12 divided by 9) and print to get your 12" block.

ADD A BORDER

If you're happy with the size of the pattern, but want or need a bigger block for your project, simply add a border to the block. Because ½" (1.3 cm) of the border will be taken up in the seam allowance (¼" [6 mm] on either side), your border will need to be larger than ½" (1.3 cm). I usually add the side borders first, and then the top and bottom. If you're feeling extra fancy, you could add a mitered-corner border. (Instructions for mitered-corner borders are not included in this book, but you can easily find resources on the Internet.)

SUBSTITUTE BLOCKS IN PROJECTS

When I was choosing which block to include for each project, I had a hard time deciding! I could have easily used the Watering Can (page 122) or the Spade and Hand Rake (page 125) for the front of the Gardening Apron (page 126). Also, the Clawfoot Bath Mat (page 84) could easily accommodate a combination of the Men's Fancy Shoe (page 61) and the Women's Fancy Shoe (page 60) as a mat for your mud room to put your shoes on.

If these thoughts are crossing your mind as well, go ahead and switch things up! Use the book to inspire you to get out of your comfort zone a little bit and alter the projects at will. Just remember, if you substitute one block for another, make sure you increase or decrease the size of it or add a border so it's the same size as the block in the original project.

REVERSE THE BLOCK

Another option to alter a block would be to reverse it. I have my personal preference for the direction the blocks face, but maybe your preference is just the opposite of mine. To reverse the blocks, use your photo-editing software or print the block as is and reverse it on a photocopier.

Bind It Up!

Several of the projects in this book feature binding. If you are unfamiliar with binding, you can find thorough treatments of the subject in general quilting books or online. Here is the basic process I use.

I try to avoid hand sewing binding at all costs because of the time it takes, plus I believe machine-sewn binding will stand up to washing and drying better than hand-sewn binding.

The first step is to machine sew the binding to the front of the project, leaving 10" (25.5 cm) tails of binding at the beginning and end. Join the two ends of binding (see the note below), finish sewing the binding to the front of the quilt, and press the binding to the back. Dab a small bead of fabric glue onto the back side of the binding, then fold and press the binding (with an iron) down just past the seam line created by sewing the binding onto the front of the quilt.

NOTE: *When I bind anything bigger than 12" (30.5 cm) or so, I always use the Binding Tool by The Quilter's Mercantile Inc. It's a big help to get those last two tails of binding diagonally sewn together without a hitch.*

Continue around the quilt in this manner, adding glue, pressing, and mitering the corners, until the binding is completely attached to the back of the quilt with glue. Then flip the quilt over to the front and stitch in the ditch around the binding seam. Most often, doing this will catch all the edges of the binding on the back of the quilt, but if you've missed a small section or two, adjust that section of binding on the back, reglue, and sew it down again from the front of the quilt.

CHAPTER 3

Kitschy Kitchen

Using things that I've made satisfies a deep longing in my heart, and since I spend time in the kitchen every day, kitchen-themed blocks and projects are favorites of mine. Although I feel like everything I make is a treasure in its own right, I make things to be used, not tucked away for a special day. I hope you will dare to do the same with these kitschy blocks and projects!

Block Key

1. Chinese Takeout Container
2. Espresso Mug
3. Oven Mitt
4. Layer Cake
5. Cast-Iron Skillet
6. Saucepan
7. Fruit Bowl

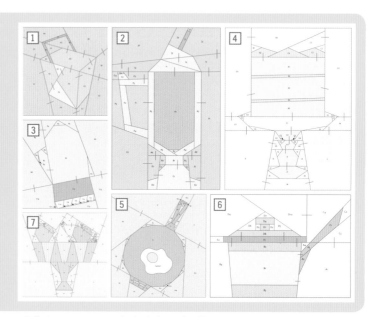

Full-size patterns are included on the CD.

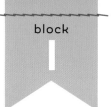

Chinese Takeout Container

Finished Size
6" × 6" (15 × 15 cm)

Fabric Needed
Black print fabric:
3" × 3" (7.5 × 7.5 cm) for handle

White fabric:
3" (7.5 × 7.5 cm) square for F2 and G1

White flower-print fabric:
7" (18 cm) square for body of box

Pink print fabric:
10" (25.5 cm) square for background

ASSEMBLE THE BLOCK

1 Print the block pattern from the CD onto foundation paper and trim close to the outside edges.

2 Cut the block into sections on the blue lines.

3 Complete all sections, leaving at least ¼" (6 mm) of fabric beyond the edges of each section. Press each section with spray starch. Trim each section ¼" (6 mm) past the pattern edges for the seam allowance.

4 Join E to D. Press toward D.

5 Join A to DE. Press toward A.

6 Join B to ADE. Press toward B.

7 Join F to G. Press toward G.

8 Join C to FG. Press seam open.

9 Join H to CFG. Press seam open.

10 Join ABDE to CFGH. Press seam open.

11 Press block with spray starch.

12 Remove the paper from the back of the block in reverse sewing order for each section.

I envision this little takeout container pieced onto the outside of a piping-clad lunch bag, with a matching napkin. I'd take it to the park to meet friends on a bright sunny day and I'd be wearing a red gingham dress and a sunhat.

Espresso Mug

Finished Size
6" × 9" (15 × 23 cm)

Fabric Needed

Black print fabric:
3" × 5" (7.5 × 12.5 cm) for coffee

White fabric:
6" (15 cm) square for mug

Off-white fabric:
4" (10 cm) square for crème

Red-and-white striped fabric:
1½" (3.8 cm) square for straw

Aqua fabric:
One fat eighth for background

ASSEMBLE THE BLOCK

1 Print the block pattern from the CD onto foundation paper and trim close to the outside edges.

2 Cut the block into sections on the blue lines.

3 Complete all sections, leaving at least ¼" (6 mm) of fabric beyond the edges of each section. Press aeach section with spray starch. Trim each section ¼" (6mm) past the pattern edges for the seam allowance.

4 Join B to C. Press seam open.

5 Join D to BC. Press seam toward D.

6 Join E to BCD. Press seam toward E.

7 Join A to BCDE. Press seam toward BCDE.

8 Join H to ABCDE. Press seam toward H.

9 Join G to F. Press seam toward F.

10 Join GF to ABCDEH. Press seam toward GF.

11 Join I to J. Press seam toward J.

12 Join IJ to ABCDEFGH. Press seam toward IJ.

13 Press block with spray starch.

14 Remove the paper from the back of the block in reverse sewing order for each section.

I am as much a morning person as a person can be. I love the quiet and watching the sun come up over the hillside. One of the very first things I do when I wake up is turn on my espresso maker for an iced latte. Because my espresso maker has a pump, it's pretty loud; when my cat hears it turn on, he comes running and wants his morning treats, too!

Oven Mitt

Finished Size
6" × 6" (15 × 15 cm)

Fabric Needed
Yellow print fabric:
5" (12.5 cm) square for body

Red print fabric:
2½" × 3½" (6.5 × 9 cm) for cuff

White solid fabric:
5" (12.5 cm) square for lace edging

Light blue fabric:
7" (18 cm) square for background

ASSEMBLE THE BLOCK

1 Print the block pattern from the CD onto foundation paper and trim close to the outside edges.

2 Cut the block into sections on the blue lines.

3 Complete all sections, leaving at least ¼" (6 mm) of fabric beyond the edges of each section. Press each section with spray starch. Trim each section ¼"(6 mm) past the pattern edges for the seam allowance.

4 Join A to B. Press seam open.

5 Join C to AB. Press seam open.

6 Press block with spray starch.

7 Remove the paper from the back of the block in reverse sewing order for each section.

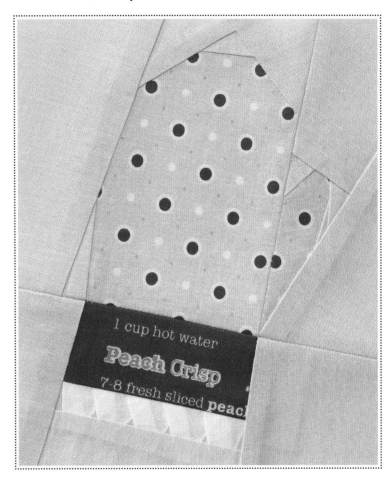

The mundane task of protecting your hand from oven heat is "prettified" with this lace-edged oven mitt. I think it would be adorable as a hot pad or pieced into a gift bag that contains gourmet baking supplies.

Layer Cake

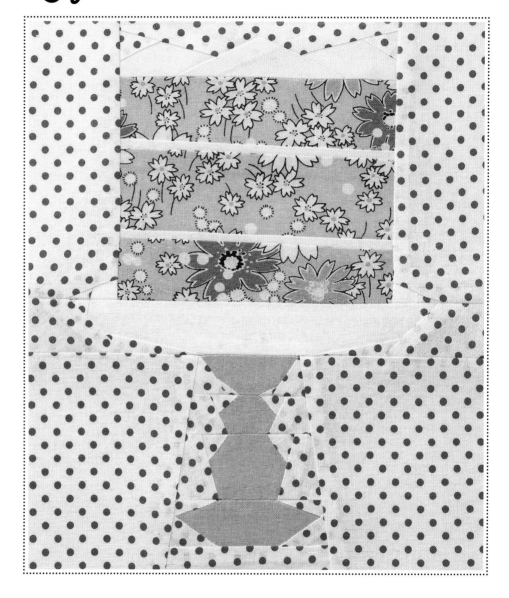

Finished Size
8" × 10" (20.5 × 25.5 cm)

Fabric Needed
Yellow flower print:
7" (18 cm) square for
cake layers

Cream fabric:
6" (15 cm) square for
frosting

White fabric:
3" × 7" (7.5 × 18 cm)
piece for cake plate

Aqua fabric:
7" (18 cm) square for
cake pedestal

**Red-and-white polka
dot fabric:**
One fat quarter for
background

A cake with a thick layer of frosting is one of my all-time favorites. In fact, once or twice a year I buy a round white cake with white frosting and eat the entire cake in two or three days. I have it for breakfast with my latte, eat a piece to supplement my lunch and dinner, and even enjoy it as a snack between meals! To keep this indulgence in check when I'm craving white cake, I've asked my husband to be a part of the decision-making process. He has helped me many a time to "step away from the cake."

ASSEMBLE THE BLOCK

1. Print the block pattern from the CD onto foundation paper and trim close to the outside edges.

2. Cut the block into sections on the blue lines.

3. Complete all sections, leaving at least ¼" (6 mm) of fabric beyond the edges of each section. Press each section with spray starch. Trim each section ¼" (6 mm) past the pattern edges for the seam allowance.

4. Join B to C. Press seam open.

5. Join A to BC. Press seam open.

6. Join D to ABC. Press seam toward D.

7. Join E to ABCD. Press seam toward E.

8. Join F to ABCDE. Press seam open.

9. Join G to H. Press seam open.

10. Join I to GH. Press seam open.

11. Join J to GHI. Press seam open.

12. Join K to GHIJ. Press seam toward K.

13. Join L to GHIJK. Press seam toward L.

14. Join ABCDEF to GHIJKL. Press seam open.

15. Press block with spray starch.

16. Remove the paper from the back of the block in reverse sewing order for each section.

Three versions of the Layer Cake block are used in the Café Pâtisserie Curtain on page 40.

Cast-Iron Skillet

Finished Size
8" × 8½" (20.5 × 21.5 cm)

Fabric Needed

Black fabric:
10" (25.5 cm) square for skillet

White fabric:
4" (10 cm) square for egg white

Yellow fabric:
2" (5 cm) square for egg yolk

Multicolored print fabric:
12" (30.5 cm) square for background

ASSEMBLE THE BLOCK

1 Print the block pattern from the CD onto foundation paper and trim close to the outside edges.

2 Cut the block into sections on the blue lines.

3 Complete all sections, leaving at least ¼" (6 mm) of fabric beyond the edges of each section. Press each section with spray starch. Trim each section ¼" (6mm) past the pattern edges for the seam allowance.

4 Join C to B. Press seam open.

5 Join D to CB. Press seam toward D.

6 Join E to BCD. Press seam toward E.

7 Join A to BCDE. Press seam open.

8 Join F to ABCDE. Press seam open.

9 Press block with spray starch.

10 Remove the paper from the back of the block in reverse sewing order for each section.

11 Print two copies of the reversed block pattern (one for the egg white appliqué and one for the egg yolk). Following appliqué instructions on page 26, appliqué first the egg white and then the yolk to the skillet.

■ *An English muffin with a fried egg is one* heck of a way to start the day, and there's no other pan that gives you a perfectly fried egg like a cast-iron skillet!

tip
Because the area is quite large, use your fabric glue stick to attach the first skillet piece to the foundation. This will ensure that it stays put while you add the surrounding areas.

Saucepan

■ *I have a small* collection of distinctive and brightly colored enamelware that I often use. This pan was inspired by that collection. It's the perfect choice for the Hot Pads project (page 50) featured later in this chapter, and inspires me while I'm in the kitchen.

Finished Size
7" × 5" (18 × 12.5 cm)

Fabric Needed

White print fabric:
4½" (11.5 cm) square for middle of pan

Light blue fabric:
6" (15 cm) square for pan bottom, handle, and lid

Black fabric:
1" × 5" (2.5 × 12.5 cm) for lid rim

Yellow-and-white checked fabric:
9" (23 cm) square for background

ASSEMBLE THE BLOCK

1 Print the block pattern from the CD onto foundation paper and trim close to the outside edges.

2 Cut the block into sections on the blue lines.

3 Complete all sections, leaving at least ¼" (6 mm) of fabric beyond the edges of each section. Press each section with spray starch. Trim each section ¼" (6 mm) past the pattern edges for the seam allowance.

4 Join A to B. Press seam open.

5 Join E to D. Press seam open.

6 Join C to DE. Press seam open.

7 Join AB to CDE. Press seam open.

8 Press block with spray starch.

9 Remove the paper from the back of the block in reverse sewing order for each section.

Fruit Bowl

I like to keep fruit in a bowl on my counter instead of in the fridge because it's just too pretty to keep hidden away. The bowl in this block is cut glass and the fruits are a patchwork of healthy living. It's the ideal block to adorn the Grocery Tote (page 44)!

Finished Size
10½" × 10" (26.5 × 25.5 cm)

Fabric Needed:

Orange fabric:
10" (25.5 cm) square for bowl foot and alternating sections

Orange-and-white checked fabric:
6" (15 cm) square for alternating print sections of bowl

Red fabric:
4" (10 cm) square for apple

Green fabric:
4" (10 cm) square for apple

Yellow fabric:
4" (10 cm) square for banana

Yellow print:
5" (12.5 cm) square for pear

Dark brown fabric:
3" (7.5 cm) square for stems

White fabric:
One fat quarter for background

ASSEMBLE THE BLOCK

1 Print the block pattern from the CD onto foundation paper and trim close to the outside edges.

2 Cut the block into sections on the blue lines.

3 Complete all sections, leaving at least ¼" (6 mm) of fabric beyond the edges of each section. Press each section with spray starch. Trim each section ¼" (6 mm) past the pattern edges for the seam allowance.

4 Join I to J. Press seam open.

5 Join K to IJ. Press seam toward K.

6 Join T to C. Press seam open.

7 Join B to CT. Press seam open.

8 Join D to BCT. Press seam open.

9 Join E to F. Press seam open.

10 Join G to H. Press seam toward H.

11 Join BCDT to EF. Press seam toward BCDT.

12 Join GH to BCDEFT. Press seam open.

13 Join IJK to BCDEFGHT. Press seam toward IJK.

14 Join L to BCDEFGHIJKT. Press seam toward L.

15 Join A to BCDEFGHIJKLT. Press seam open.

16 Join M to ABCDEFGHIJKLT. Press seam toward M.

17 Join N to ABCDEFGHIJKLMT. Press seam toward N.

18 Join P to O. Press seam toward O.

19 Join Q to OP. Press seam open.

20 Join R to OPQ. Press seam toward R.

21 Join S to OPQR. Press seam toward S.

22 Join ABCDEFGHIJKLMNT to OPQRS. Press seam open.

23 Press block with spray starch.

24 Remove the paper from the back of the block in reverse sewing order for each section.

The Fruit Bowl block is used on the Grocery Tote (page 44)

CAFÉ PÂTISSERIE CURTAIN

This curtain will make you smile with its cheery vibe and will lift your spirits each and every time you find yourself at the sink washing dishes. On the other hand, if you look at it too long, you just might skip the dishes and go right to baking a cake instead!

featured block
Layer Cake (page 34)

finished size
46" × 13¾" (117 × 35 cm), including hanging tabs

Notes

▶ This curtain is designed to be 46" (117 cm) wide. If you'd like to make the curtain smaller, reduce the width of the plain-fabric panels at each end. In other words, if you want the curtain to be 36" (91.5 cm) wide, you would reduce the width of the plain-fabric pieces by 5" (12.5 cm) each, for a total of 10" (25.5 cm). Remember to resize the backing as well. You can also make the curtain wider by increasing the width of the plain-fabric panels.

▶ You can also add or subtract pieced blocks to make a custom-size curtain for your window, adjusting the fabric requirements as needed.

Fabric

- Fabrics for 3 Layer Cake blocks as listed on page 34
- 1½ yd (137 cm) of white fabric for curtain front and Layer Cake backgrounds
- 1⅜ yd (128 cm) of muslin for curtain backing
- One fat quarter of red-and-white diagonal check for hanging loops and pieced diamonds

Other Materials

- Three copies of the Layer Cake block pattern (on CD)
- Two copies of the diamond block pattern (on CD)
- Café Pâtisserie embroidery pattern (page 132)

Tools

- Saral transfer paper
- Embossing tool or pencil
- 6-strand embroidery floss (red used in the sample) and needle

CUT THE FABRIC

From the white fabric, cut:

- ▶ 2 side panels, 8½" × 13" (21.5 × 33 cm)
- ▶ 2 diamond-top panels, 3½" × 4" (9 × 10 cm)
- ▶ 2 diamond-bottom panels, 3½" × 5" (9 × 12.5 cm)
- ▶ 1 bottom panel, 3½" × 30½" (9 × 77.5cm)
- ▶ 5 hanging tabs, 2½" × 3½" (6.5 × 9 cm)

From the muslin, cut on lengthwise grain:

- ▶ 1 backing panel, 13" × 46½" (33 × 118 cm)

From the red diagonal check, cut:

- ▶ 5 hanging tabs, 2½" × 3½" (6.5 × 9 cm)

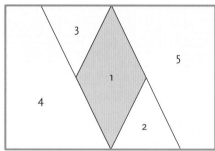

The full-size diamond block pattern is included on the CD.

DIRECTIONS

❶ Piece and assemble three Layer Cakes (page 34) and two diamond blocks.

❷ Following the assembly diagram, assemble the curtain front. Sew the diamond-top and diamond-bottom panels to the diamond blocks' top and bottom edges, and then sew the diamond panels between the Layer Cake blocks. Sew the bottom panel to the lower edge of the assembly. Finish the curtain front by sewing a side panel to each end of the assembled section.

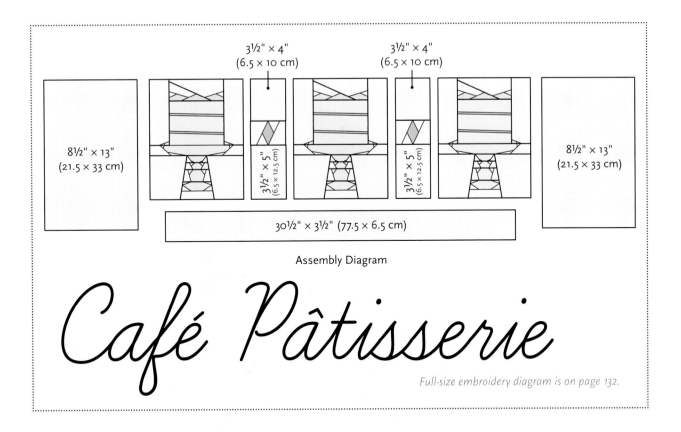

3½" × 4"
(6.5 × 10 cm)

3½" × 4"
(6.5 × 10 cm)

8½" × 13"
(21.5 × 33 cm)

3½" × 5"
(6.5 × 12.5 cm)

3½" × 5"
(6.5 × 12.5 cm)

8½" × 13"
(21.5 × 33 cm)

30½" × 3½" (77.5 × 6.5 cm)

Assembly Diagram

Café Pâtisserie

Full-size embroidery diagram is on page 132.

3 Transfer the Café Pâtisserie embroidery diagram onto the lower panel in the area under the cakes as explained on page 24.

4 Embroider the words using a backstitch and embroidery floss (3 strands were used in the sample).

5 With right sides together, layer one checked hanging tab on a white tab and sew the 3½" (9 cm) edges. Turn the tube right side out and press the tab flat. Repeat to make five tabs.

6 With the front side of the curtain right side up, fold the hanging tabs in half cross-wise and lay them along the top of the curtain front, with the tabs' raw edges extending ⅜" (3 mm) beyond the raw edge of the curtain top. Position one tab at the center of the

curtain and two additional tabs, each 1½" (3.8 cm) from the curtain side edges. Space the remaining tabs evenly between the side and center tabs. Pin the hanging tabs to the curtain and baste ⅛" (3 mm) from the upper raw edge.

7 With right sides together, layer the curtain front and muslin backing. Sew around the edges, leaving a 3" (7.5 cm) gap in the bottom seam for turning.

8 Trim the corners diagonally to reduce bulk. Turn the curtain right side out and press, turning the raw edges to the inside along the gap.

9 Hand stitch the opening closed.

10 Topstitch ¼" (6 mm) from the curtain edges.

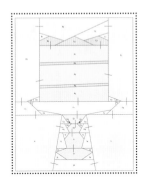

See the CD for the full-size block pattern.

GROCERY TOTE

Making earth-friendly choices brings me happiness, so I take my own shopping bags to the grocery store. I designed this tote bag to be extra wide for carrying those large items that don't fit in ordinary grocery bags, like frozen pizzas!

featured block
Fruit Bowl (page 38)

finished size
16½" × 21" (42 × 53.5 cm), excluding handles

Fabric

■ Fabrics for Fruit Bowl block as listed on page 38

■ 1¼ yd (114.5 cm) of tan fabric for outside of bag

■ 1 yd (91.5 cm) of print fabric for lining

■ ½ yd (45.5 cm) of blue-and-white print fabric for binding and handles

Other Supplies

■ 1 copy of the Fruit Bowl block pattern (on CD)

CUT THE FABRIC

From the tan fabric, cut:

▶ 2 side panels, 23¼" × 17" (59 × 43 cm)

▶ 1 top panel, 3¼" × 11" (8.5 × 28 cm)

▶ 1 bottom panel, 4¼" × 11" (11 × 28 cm)

From the lining fabric, cut:

▶ 2 pieces, 28½" × 17" (72.5 × 43 cm)

From the blue-and-white print, cut:

▶ 2 strips, 2½" (6.5 cm) × width of fabric

▶ 2 strips, 25½" × 4" (65 × 10 cm) each for medium-length handles or 30" × 4" (76 × 10 cm) each for long handles

DIRECTIONS

❶ Piece and assemble one Fruit Bowl block (page 38).

❷ Following the diagram, assemble the bag body. Sew the top and bottom panels to the pieced block, and then sew a side panel to each side of the block.

❸ Fold the outside bag body in half, right sides together, aligning the 17" (43 cm) edges at the center back, and stitch to make a tube.

❹ Place the lining rectangles right sides together and sew both 17" (43 cm) edges, forming a tube.

❺ Place the outside bag tube inside the lining tube, wrong sides together. Position the center back seam of the bag body at the midpoint of one lining rectangle; the lining seams will be at the sides of the bag. Fold the bag and lining in half at the side seams so that the bag body is right sides together and the center back seam meets the center front of the bag.

Note: It is helpful to use a walking foot for the following steps.

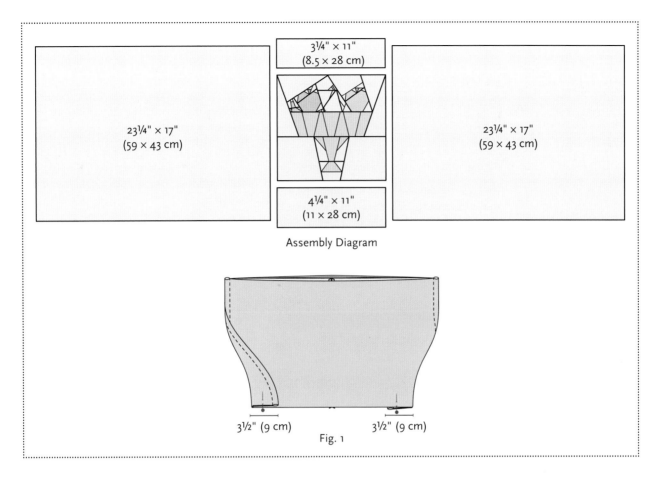

3¼" × 11"
(8.5 × 28 cm)

23¼" × 17"
(59 × 43 cm)

23¼" × 17"
(59 × 43 cm)

4¼" × 11"
(11 × 28 cm)

Assembly Diagram

3½" (9 cm)   3½" (9 cm)

Fig. 1

6 Pin the folded bag and lining together along the side seams and sew a ½" (1.3 cm) seam down each side. Double stitching the side seams in this way creates a sturdy and attractive finish similar to a French seam.

7 Measure 3½" (9 cm) from the edge of the right side seam allowance at the bottom of the bag and mark with a pin. Fold the right edge of the bag toward the bag back at the pin. Align the bottom raw edges and pin the fold in place **(fig. 1)**.

8 Repeat Step 7 on the left side of the bag, but fold the bag toward the bag front.

9 Sew a ⅜" (1 cm) seam along the bag bottom, backstitching at the beginning and end of the seam.

10 Turn the bag right side out and use a tool to make sure the bottom corners are fully turned.

11 Fold the bag flat along the sides, matching the center front and back. Sew a ½" (1.3 cm) seam along the bottom of the turned bag, enclosing the previous seam allowances.

12 Sew the two blue-and-white 2½" (6.5 cm) × width of fabric strips together along the 2½" (6.5 cm) edges of the strips. Press the seam allowances open and trim the strip to 54½" (138.5 cm) for binding.

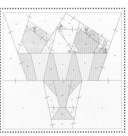

See the CD for the full-size block pattern.

13 Sew the remaining two short ends of the binding strip together to form a tube. Press the binding in half, wrong sides together, aligning the raw edges.

14 Pin the prepared binding to the lining side of the bag, matching the raw edges at the top of the bag and folding the side-seam allowances toward the bag back. Sew the binding to the bag with a ⅜" (1 cm) seam allowance.

15 Press the binding to the outside of the bag so the folded edge of the binding just covers the seam and pin. Edgestitch the binding fold, enclosing the raw edges.

16 Lay the bag flat and extend the side folds from the bottom seam to the upper edge, creating pleats at the sides of the bag. Pin the four folds, and then topstitch ½" (1.3 cm) from the side edge of each fold, from the upper edge to the topstitching along the bottom seam (**figs. 2 and 3**).

17 Press ½" (1.3) cm to the wrong side on all four edges of one handle strip. Fold the strip in half lengthwise, wrong sides together, and press (**fig. 4**).

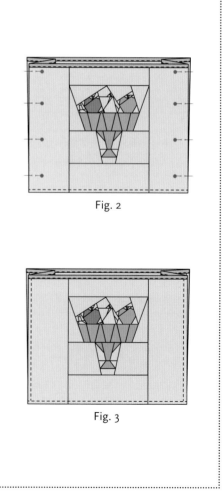

Fig. 2

Fig. 3

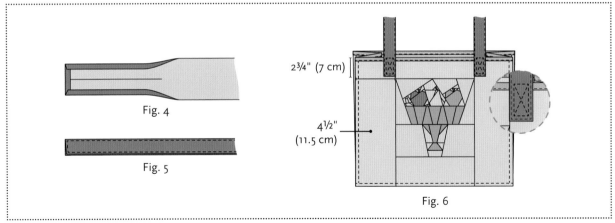

Fig. 4

Fig. 5

2¾" (7 cm)

4½" (11.5 cm)

Fig. 6

18 Pin the pressed handle edges together and topstitch ¼" (6 mm) from all four edges **(fig. 5)**. Repeat Steps 17 and 18 to make a second handle.

19 Position one end of a prepared handle on the bag front, 4½" (11.5 cm) from the top-stitched side edge of the bag, with the end of the handle 2¾" (7 cm) below the top of the bag, and pin. Sew again over the handle topstitching and continue stitching across the handle at the bag's upper edge, and then stitch an × on each handle end to reinforce. Repeat to attach both ends of each handle, sewing one handle to the bag front and the other to the bag back **(fig. 6)**.

tip
This is a big bag that will accommodate larger grocery purchases. If you'd like to make it smaller, I would recommend reducing the width but not the height.

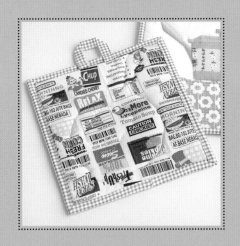

HOT PADS

I like to keep a supply of hot pads on hand for last-minute gifts. These two contain a layer of Insul-Bright, an insulating batting that helps reflect the heat away from your hand. Make sure the shiny side of the Insul-Bright is facing the undecorated side of the hot pad (the side that will come into contact with hot pans). These practical hot pads are constructed so they can be used frequently and thrown in the wash when soiled.

featured blocks
Cast-Iron Skillet (page 36), Saucepan (page 37)

finished size
8½" × 8¾" (21.5 × 22 cm) each, excluding hanger

Fabric for One Hot Pad

- Fabrics for Cast-Iron Skillet block (as listed on page 36) or Saucepan block (page 37)
- Red-and-white check: 1 strip 2½" (6.5 cm) × width of fabric for binding and tab
- Multicolored print: 10" (25.5 cm) square for backing
- Red-and-white flower print: 8½" × 4¼" (21.5 × 11 cm) rectangle for saucepan hot pad

Other Supplies

- 1 copy of Saucepan block pattern or Cast-Iron Skillet block pattern, plus 2 copies of reversed block pattern for appliqué (on CD)
- 10" (25.5 cm) square cotton batting
- 10" (25.5 cm) square Insul-Bright
- 6-strand embroidery floss (white used in the sample) and needle for Cast-Iron Skillet block
- Water-soluble, fabric-safe glue

Tools

Walking foot

DIRECTIONS

Saucepan Hot Pad

1. Piece the Saucepan block (page 37).

2. Cut two 1" × 5½" (2.5 × 14 cm) strips from the leftover background fabric. Sew one to each side of the pieced block.

3. Sew the 8¼" × 4¼" (21.5 × 11 cm) rectangle of floral fabric to the bottom edge of the assembled unit.

4. Layer the backing fabric, right side down; the Insul-Bright, shiny side down; the batting; and the Saucepan block, right side up. Baste with pins.

5. Echo quilt ⅛" (3 mm) outside the pan.

6. Trim the batting and backing to match the hot pad top.

7. Fold the binding fabric in half lengthwise, wrong sides together, and press.

8. Working from the right side of the hot pad, align the raw edges of the binding with the bottom raw edge, beginning at the right of center, and place a pin about 1½" (3.8 cm) from the lower left corner (**fig. 1**).

9. Sew the binding to the hot pad, using a walking foot and mitering the corners as you go. Begin sewing at the pin, leaving the binding tail free.

10. Continue sewing around the hot pad to a point about 1½" (3.8 cm) past the lower right (last) corner.

11. Fold the binding tails back on themselves so their folded edges touch, and then press the folds (**fig. 2**).

12. Trim the excess binding from each end, leaving a ¼" (6 mm) seam allowance past the folds (**fig. 3**).

13. Open the folded binding ends. Align the folds from Step 11, right sides together and raw edges matched; pin and sew along the fold line (**figs. 4 and 5**).

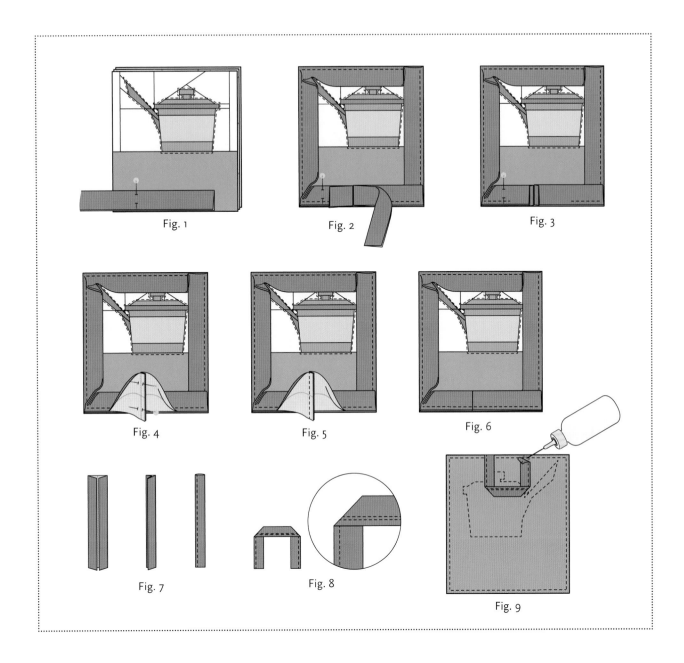

Fig. 1

Fig. 2

Fig. 3

Fig. 4

Fig. 5

Fig. 6

Fig. 7

Fig. 8

Fig. 9

⑭ Press the seam allowances open and refold the binding. Finish sewing it to the bottom edge of the hot pad **(fig. 6)**.

⑮ Cut a 5¾" (14.5 cm)-long strip of leftover binding. Open the crease and fold both long edges to the wrong side so they meet at the center crease and press. Refold along the center crease and press again. Edgestitch the long open edge to close the strip **(fig. 7)**.

⑯ Fold the loop as shown in **fig. 8** and sew over the edgestitching again, across the base of the horizontal section, holding the layers together.

⑰ Position the loop on the hot pad wrong side, centered on the top edge, with the raw edges matched. Use a few drops of water-soluble glue to baste the loop in place **(fig. 9)**.

tip

For extra heat protection, use heavier-weight home-décor fabric for the backing and/or two layers of cotton batting in addition to the Insul-Bright.

⑱ Turn the binding to the wrong side and press, and then use a thin line of water-soluble glue to tack the binding in place, just covering the binding seam **(fig. 10)**.

⑲ Turn the hot pad over and stitch in the ditch along the binding, catching the free edge of the binding and the hanging loop in the seam.

⑳ Flip the loop up, across the binding, and sew it in place along the outer edge of the binding **(fig. 11)**.

Cast-Iron Skillet Hot Pad

❶ Piece and appliqué the Cast-Iron Skillet block (page 36).

❷ Layer the backing fabric, right side down; the Insul-Bright, shiny side down; the batting; and the Cast-Iron Skillet block, right side up. Baste with pins.

❸ Echo quilt ⅛" (3 mm) outside the skillet.

❹ Use two strands of embroidery floss to quilt a running stitch around the egg white.

❺ Follow Steps 6–20 for the Saucepan Hot Pad to finish the Cast-Iron Skillet Hot Pad.

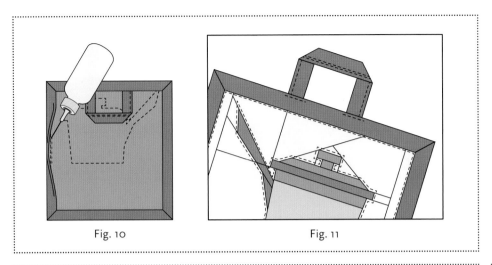

Fig. 10   Fig. 11

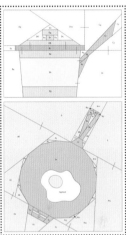

See the CD for the full-size block patterns.

CHAPTER 4

Wear It!

My taste in clothes runs toward simple, fitted, flattering clothing with a touch of crazy thrown in to balance things out. I drew from that philosophy to create the clothing-inspired blocks in the following pages. Use the blocks to adorn clothespin holders, tote bags, pillows, or the shoe keepers featured in this chapter—use your imagination!

Block Key

8 Bathing Suit

9 Sleeveless Dress

10 T-shirt

11 Women's Fancy Shoe

12 Men's Fancy Shoe

13 Those 70s Pants

14 Beach Bag

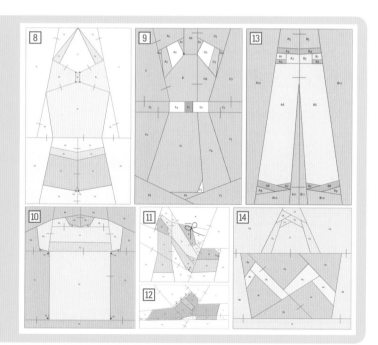

Full-size patterns are included on the CD.

Bathing Suit

Finished Size
8" × 13" (20.5 × 33 cm)

Fabric Needed

Multicolored stripe fabric:
7" (18 cm) square for shorts

Pink print fabric:
10" (25.5 cm) square for top

Pink fabric:
4" (10 cm) square for ties, bust center, and waistband

White fabric:
One fat eighth for background

ASSEMBLE THE BLOCK

1 Print the block pattern from the CD onto foundation paper and trim close to the outside edges.

2 Cut the block into sections on the blue lines.

3 Complete all sections, leaving at least ¼" (6 mm) of fabric beyond the edges of each section. Press each section with spray starch. Trim each section ¼" (6 mm) past the pattern edges for the seam allowance.

Note: There are two Y-seams in this block (between A and B, and between B and C), so do not sew past the edge of the pattern on the sewing lines with green dots. Backstitch at the pattern edge instead.

4 Join A to B using instructions for Y-seams on page 23. Press seam toward B.

5 Join AB to C using instructions for Y-seams. Press seam toward B.

6 Join D to ABC. Press toward D.

7 Join E to ABCD. Press toward E.

8 Join F to G. Press seam open.

9 Join ABCDE to FG. Press seam open.

10 Press block with spray starch.

11 Remove the paper from the back of the block in reverse sewing order for each section.

This pinup-style swimsuit reminds me of Elly May from *The Beverly Hillbillies*. It has a simple, clean look, but its construction has two Y-seams, so be sure to read about Y-seams on page 23 before you start. Y-seams are simple, but they require a few special steps.

Sleeveless Dress

Finished Size

5" × 8" (12.5 × 20.5 cm)

Fabric Needed

Aqua fabric:
7" (18 cm) square for dress

White fabric:
5" (12.5 cm) square for collar, belt, and skirt detail

Medium blue fabric:
1" (2.5 cm) square for center of belt

Black-and-white text-print fabric:
8" (20.5 cm) square for background

ASSEMBLE THE BLOCK

❶ Print the block pattern from the CD onto foundation paper and trim close to the outside edges.

❷ Cut the block into sections on the blue lines.

❸ Complete all sections, leaving ¼" (6 mm) of fabric beyond the edges of each section. Press each section with spray starch. Trim each section ¼" (6 mm) past the pattern edges for the seam allowance.

Note: There is a Y-seam between A and B, so do not sew past the edge of the pattern on the sewing lines with green dots. Backstitch at the pattern edge instead.

❹ Join A to B, following the instructions for Y-seams on page 23. Press toward B.

❺ Join C to AB. Press toward C.

❻ Join D to ABC. Press toward ABC.

❼ Join E to ABCD. Press toward E.

❽ Join F to ABCDE. Press toward E.

❾ Press block with spray starch.

❿ Remove the paper from the back of the block in reverse sewing order for each section.

This little dress, with its off-center front seam, oversized collar, and wide belt has a mod vibe. I think it would be super cute in a printed fabric, too!

T-shirt

Finished Size
7½" × 8" (19 × 20.5 cm)

Fabric Needed
Pale green fabric:
9" (23 cm) square for T-shirt

Lavender print fabric:
5" × 2" (12.5 × 5 cm) for accent

Pink print fabric:
One fat sixteenth for background

ASSEMBLE THE BLOCK

1 Print the block pattern from the CD onto foundation paper and trim close to the outside edges.

2 Cut the block into sections on the blue lines.

3 Complete all sections, leaving at least ¼" (6 mm) of fabric beyond the edges of each section. Press each section with spray starch. Trim each section ¼" (6 mm) past the pattern edges for the seam allowance.

4 Join A to B. Press seam open.

5 Join C to AB. Press seam open.

6 Join D to ABC. Press seam toward D.

7 Join E to ABCD. Press seam toward E.

8 Join G to F. Press seam toward F.

9 Join H to FG. Press seam toward H.

10 Join ABCDE to FGH. Press seam open.

11 Press block with spray starch.

12 Remove the paper from the back of the block in reverse sewing order for each section.

The horizontal strip on this simple T-shirt reminds me of workout clothes from the 70s. It's the perfect spot to add a little fussy cutting. Follow the instructions on page 21 to align your fussy-cut fabric correctly.

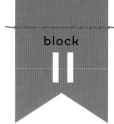
Women's Fancy Shoe

The perfect complement to the Men's Fancy Shoe, this female counterpart is comfortable and stylish with just the right amount of flair. I would wear these shoes in a heartbeat.

Finished Size
8" × 6½" (20.5 × 16.5 cm)

Fabric Needed
Orange plaid fabric:
10" (25.5 cm) square for heel and sole

Aqua fabric:
7" (18 cm) square for shoe detail

Polka dot fabric:
7" (18 cm) square for shoe upper

Light brown fabric:
One fat eighth for background

Other Supplies
Embroidery floss for shoelace (black used in the sample)

ASSEMBLE THE BLOCK

1 Print the block pattern from the CD onto foundation paper and trim close to the outside edges.

2 Cut the block into sections on the blue lines.

3 Complete all sections, leaving at least ¼" (6 mm) of fabric beyond the edges of each section. Press each section with spray starch. Trim each section ¼" (6mm) past the pattern edges for the seam allowance.

4 Join F to G. Press seam open.

5 Join FG to D. Press seam open.

6 Join B to C. Press seam open.

7 Join BC to DFG. Press seam open.

8 Join E to BCDFG. Press seam open.

9 Join A to BCDEFG. Press seam open.

10 Press block with spray starch.

11 Remove the paper from the back of the block in reverse sewing order for each section.

12 Print a copy of the reversed block pattern. Following the instructions on page 24, transfer the shoelace to the pieced block and embroider with a backstitch.

Men's Fancy Shoe

■ *Thank you to Robert* Blackard of Rob and Bob Studio for permission to turn his men's shoe illustration into this shoe block. It's the perfect shoe for the hipster on the go!

Finished Size
10½" × 5" (26.5 × 12.5 cm)

Fabric Needed
Dark brown print fabric:
5" (12.5 cm) square for heel and sole

Red print fabric:
8" (20.5 cm) square for shoe

Blue fabric:
3" (7.5 cm) square for shoe detail

Blue pin-dot fabric:
10" (25.5 cm) square for background

ASSEMBLE THE BLOCK

1 Print the block pattern from the CD onto foundation paper and trim close to the outside edges.

2 Cut the block into sections on the blue lines.

3 Complete all sections, leaving at least ¼" (6 mm) of fabric beyond the edges of each section. Press each section with spray starch. Trim each section ¼" (6 mm) past the pattern edges for the seam allowance.

4 Join A to B. Press seam open.

5 Join C to D. Press seam open.

6 Join E to CD. Press seam open.

7 Join AB to CDE. Press seam open.

8 Join F to G. Press seam open.

9 Join ABCDE to FG. Press seam open.

10 Press block with spray starch.

11 Remove the paper from the back of the block in reverse sewing order for each section.

Those 70s Pants

Finished Size
4" × 6½" (10 × 16.5 cm)

Fabric Needed
Multicolored plaid fabric:
7" (18 cm) square for pants

Red fabric:
4" (10 cm) square for accent

Orange fabric:
9" (23 cm) square for background

ASSEMBLE THE BLOCK

1 Print the block pattern from the CD onto foundation paper and trim close to the outside edges.

2 Cut the block into sections on the blue lines.

3 Complete all sections, leaving at least ¼" (6 mm) of fabric beyond the edges of each section. Press each section with spray starch. Trim each section ¼" (6mm) past the pattern edges for the seam allowance.

4 Join A to B. Press seam open.

5 Press block with spray starch.

6 Remove the paper from the back of the block in reverse sewing order for each section.

■ *Seventies disco dance party.*
That's all I'm gonna say.

Beach Bag

The beach bag block is the perfect tagalong to the Bathing Suit block (page 57). In fact, they would make a fabulous pair next to each other on a summery tote.

Finished Size
7" × 7" (18 × 18 cm)

Fabric Needed
Pink floral fabric:
8" (20.5 cm) square for bag

Yellow fabric:
5" (12.5 cm) square for zigzag accent

Pink fabric:
4" (10 cm) square for handle

Green-and-white print fabric:
One fat sixteenth for background

ASSEMBLE THE BLOCK

1. Print the block pattern from the CD onto foundation paper and trim close to the outside edges.

2. Cut the block into sections on the blue lines.

3. Complete all sections, leaving at least ¼" (6 mm) of fabric beyond the edges of each section. Press each section with spray starch. Trim each section ¼" (6 mm) past the pattern edges for the seam allowance.

4. Join A to B. Press seam open.

5. Join C to AB. Press seam toward C.

6. Join D to ABC. Press seam toward ABC.

7. Press block with spray starch.

8. Remove the paper from the back of the block in reverse sewing order for each section.

HIS AND HERS SHOE KEEPERS

These bags will protect your favorite pairs of shoes, whether in your closet (from your pets) or while you travel. The bags have a divided lining to keep the shoes from bumping together and scuffing and a zip top to keep them contained. I mixed it up a bit by free motion stitching the bow on the women's fancy shoe block with my machine instead of stitching it by hand. The words "His" and "Hers" are printed on the fabric for a fun way to keep things straight.

featured blocks
Women's Fancy Shoe (page 60), Men's Fancy Shoe (page 61)

finished sizes
Hers: 14 ½" × 17" (37 × 43 cm), His: 18" × 17 ¾" (45.5 × 45 cm)

Fabric for Hers

- Fabrics for Women's Fancy Shoe block on page 60
- ½ yd (45.5 cm) of off-white fabric
- ½ yd (45.5 cm) of print fabric for lining
- ¼ yd (23 cm) of gray gingham

Other Supplies for Hers

- Woman's Fancy Shoe block pattern, plus reversed block pattern for embroidery (on CD)
- 16" (40.5 cm) zipper
- 13" (33 cm) of ½" (1.3 cm) wide cotton or twill tape
- "HERS" template (on CD)

Fabric for His

- Fabrics for Men's Fancy Shoe block on page 61
- ⅝ yd (57.5 cm) of off-white fabric
- ⅝ yd (57.5 cm) of print fabric
- ¼ yd (23 cm) of gray gingham

Other Supplies for His

- Men's Fancy Shoe block pattern (on CD)
- 20" (51 cm) zipper
- 13" (33 cm) of ½" (1.3 cm) wide twill tape
- "HIS" template (on CD)

Tools

- Bubble Jet Set 2000 & Bubble Jet Set Rinse
- Inkjet Printer
- Chalk marker
- Freezer paper
- Walking foot
- Saral transfer paper, embossing tool (for shoelace embroidery for Hers)
- Water-soluble, fabric-safe glue

CUT THE FABRIC FOR HERS

From the off-white fabric, cut:

- ▶ 1 bag back, 14½" × 17½" (37 × 44.5 cm)
- ▶ 1 upper front, 6 ¾" × 14½" (17 × 37 cm)
- ▶ 2 side fronts, 3¾" × 11 ¼" (9.5 × 28.5 cm)
- ▶ 1 printed panel*, 4¾" × 8½" (12 × 21.5 cm)

From the print fabric, cut:

- ▶ 2 lining rectangles, 14½" × 17½" (37 × 44.5 cm)

From the gray gingham, cut:

- ▶ 2 binding strips, 2" (5 cm) × width of fabric; sew together and trim to measure 2" × 55" (5 × 139.5 cm)
- ▶ 2 zipper tabs, 2½" × 2½" (6.5 × 6.5 cm)

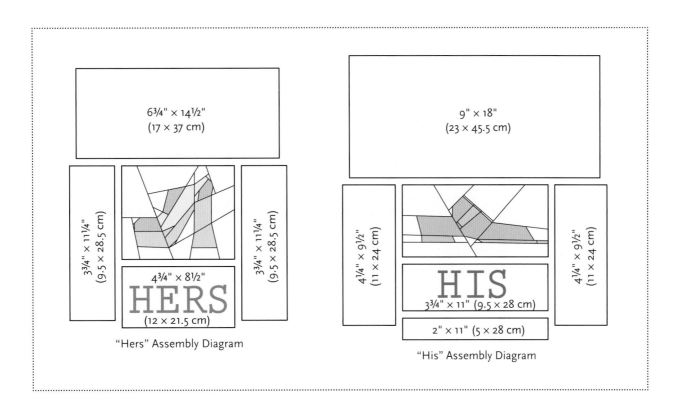

6¾" × 14½"
(17 × 37 cm)

3¾" × 11¼"
(9.5 × 28.5 cm)

3¾" × 11¼"
(9.5 × 28.5 cm)

4¾" × 8½"

HERS

(12 × 21.5 cm)

"Hers" Assembly Diagram

9" × 18"
(23 × 45.5 cm)

4¼" × 9½"
(11 × 24 cm)

4¼" × 9½"
(11 × 24 cm)

HIS

3¾" × 11" (9.5 × 28 cm)

2" × 11" (5 × 28 cm)

"His" Assembly Diagram

CUT THE FABRIC FOR HIS

From the off-white fabric, cut:

- ▸ 1 bag back, 18" × 18" (45.5 × 45.5 cm)
- ▸ 1 upper front, 9" × 18" (23 × 45.5 cm)
- ▸ 2 side fronts, 4¼" × 9½" (11 × 24 cm)
- ▸ 1 printed panel*, 3¾" × 11" (9.5 × 28 cm)
- ▸ 1 lower front, 2" × 11" (5 × 28 cm)

From the print fabric, cut:

- ▸ 2 lining squares, 18" × 18"
  (45.5 × 45.5 cm)

From the gray gingham, cut:

- ▸ 2 binding strips, 2" (5 cm) × width of
  fabric; sew the strips together and trim
  to 2" × 65" (5 × 165 cm)
- ▸ 2 zipper tabs, 2½" × 2½" (6.5 × 6.5 cm)

*Cut these pieces oversize and trim after
printing.

DIRECTIONS (FOR EITHER KEEPER)

1 Piece shoe block following the
instructions for either the Women's Fancy
Shoe (page 60) or the Men's Fancy Shoe
(page 61).

2 Following the manufacturer's instructions
for Bubble Jet Set 2000 and Jet Set Rinse,
print "HIS" or "HERS" from the file on the CD
onto the off-white fabric. Trim the panel to
size when the printing process is complete.

3 Refer to the assembly diagrams to assemble the front of the bag. Sew the bottom
section(s) onto the shoe block. Attach the
sides, and then add the top panel.

4 Center the zipper on the upper edge of the
bag front, right sides together, with the edge
of the zipper tape along the bag's raw edge.
Place one lining piece on top, with the lining
right side against the zipper's wrong side,
and the raw edges of the lining and bag front

matched. The zipper pull should be toward the left edge of the bag front. Pin in place (**fig. 1**).

5 Mark the top edge of the lining fabric ¾" (2 cm) in from each side.

6 Using a zipper foot, sew ⅛" (3 mm) from the zipper teeth between the marks made in Step 5. Backstitch the seam at the beginning and end.

7 Turn the pieces right side out with the lining on the bottom and the bag front right side up. Press the layers away from the zipper, continuing to press the seam allowances to the wrong side all the way to the side edges. Edgestitch the seam between marks.

8 Repeat Steps 5–7 with the second lining piece and the bag back, aligning the front and back pieces across the zipper tape.

9 Position the lining pieces with right sides together, leaving the bag front and back free. Glue baste the twill tape down the center of the back lining. Sew along the center of the tape through both lining pieces, backstitching at both ends of the seam (**fig. 2**).

10 Smooth the bag front and back into position on the lining, wrong sides together, aligning the raw edges. Pin together, pulling the zipper ends up so that the raw edges of the fabrics next to the zipper ends can be pinned.

11 Fold the binding in half lengthwise, wrong sides together, and press.

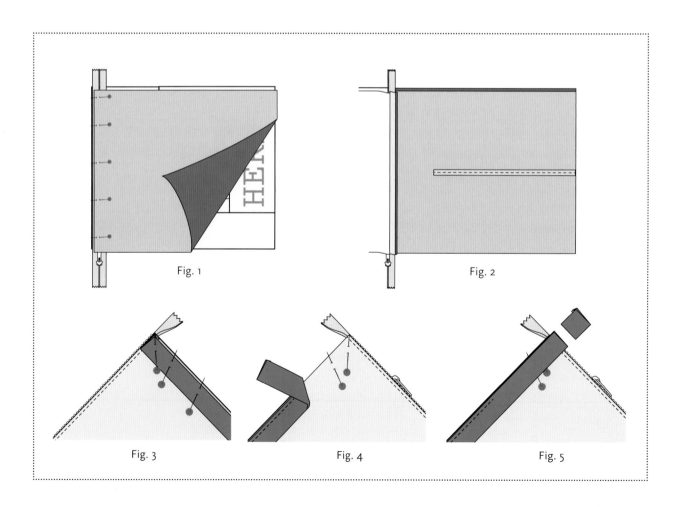

Fig. 1

Fig. 2

Fig. 3

Fig. 4

Fig. 5

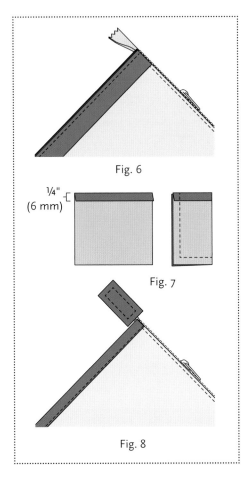

Fig. 6

¼"
(6 mm)

Fig. 7

Fig. 8

⑫ Unfold the binding and press ¼" (6 mm) to the wrong side on one short end. Refold the first crease and press again.

⑬ Align the folded end of the binding with the pressed seam allowances at one end of the zipper and sew the binding to the bag, matching the raw edges of the binding and bag and leaving the zipper free. Use a walking foot if desired. Miter the lower corners as you go and stop sewing about 3" (7.5 cm) from the zipper on the opposite side **(figs. 3 and 4)**.

⑭ Trim the binding so it extends ¼" (6 mm) beyond the pressed seam allowances at the end of the zipper. Unfold the binding and press ¼" (6 mm) to the wrong side on the short end. Refold and press again. Pin the binding to the bag and finish stitching, again leaving the zipper free **(figs. 5 and 6)**.

⑮ Press the binding to the back of the bag, enclosing the raw edges, and glue baste the binding fold so it covers the seam line.

⑯ From the front of the bag, topstitch the binding ⅛" (3 mm) from the seam line to catch the binding on the bag back.

⑰ Press ¼" (6 mm) to the wrong side on one edge of a zipper tab. Fold the tab lengthwise with the right sides together, and sew the long edge and the unfinished short end **(fig. 7)**.

⑱ Trim the corners diagonally and turn the tab right side out. Slide it over one end of the zipper so the pressed edge is close to the bag body and topstitch ¼" (6 mm) from all four tab edges, attaching the tab to the end of the zipper **(fig. 8)**. Repeat Steps 17 and 18 to make and attach the second tab.

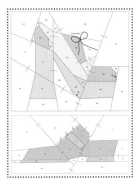

See the CD for the full-size block patterns.

CHAPTER 5

Retro Home

I don't need a lot of stuff for a cozy home: a chair, a phone, a couch, a footstool, a lamp, and a TV. What else do you need? The funky furnishings in this chapter will liven up any dwelling. In addition to the featured pillow and bath mat projects, I can see these blocks in a wall quilt or table runners, or simply framed and hung on the wall.

Block Key

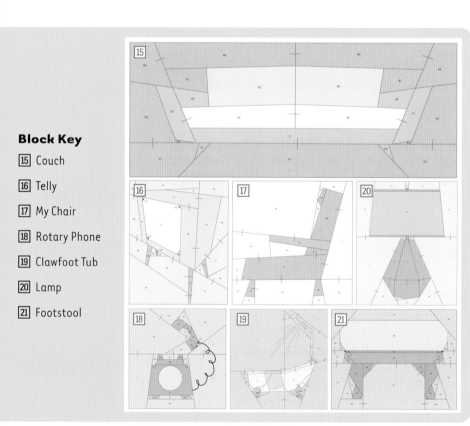

Full-size patterns are included on the CD.

Couch

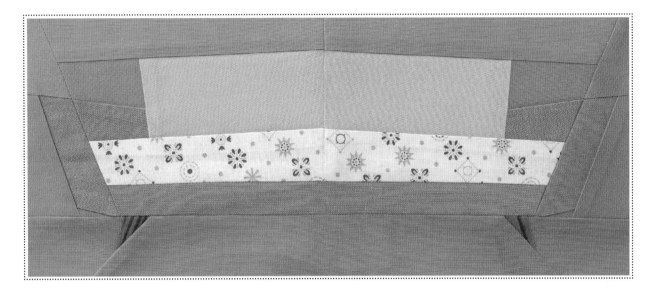

▨ *If I saw this couch for sale* somewhere, I'd buy it in a heartbeat. It would be fabulous in a solid fabric or with one print, or mixed up as I've done in this block. It has a simple construction; just make sure to get those center seams aligned for a clean look once it's pieced!

Finished Size
15" × 6" (38 × 15 cm)

Fabric Needed
Woodgrain print fabric:
2" (5 cm) square for feet

Aqua fabric:
11" × 4" (28 × 10 cm) for arms and base

Light blue fabric:
5" (12.5 cm) square for back cushions

Print fabric:
4" × 6" (10 × 15 cm) for seat cushions

Orange fabric:
One fat eighth for background

ASSEMBLE THE BLOCK

1 Print the block pattern from the CD onto foundation paper and trim close to the outside edges.

2 Cut the block into sections on the blue lines.

3 Complete all sections, leaving at least ¼" (6 mm) of fabric beyond the edges of each section. Press each section with spray starch. Trim each section ¼" (6 mm) past the pattern edges for the seam allowance.

4 Join A to B. Press seam open.

5 Join C to AB. Press seam toward AB.

6 Join E to ABC. Press seam open.

7 Join D to ABCE. Press seam open.

8 Join F to G. Press seam toward F.

9 Join ABCDE to FG. Press seam open.

10 Press block with spray starch.

11 Remove the paper from the back of the block in reverse sewing order for each section.

Telly

Finished Size
7" × 8½" (18 × 21.5 cm)

Fabric Needed
Text-print fabric:
4" (10 cm) square for screen

Dark aqua fabric:
7" (18 cm) square for TV cabinet

Brown print fabric:
3" (7.5 cm) square for legs

Multicolored floral fabric:
12" (30.5 cm) square for background

ASSEMBLE THE BLOCK
1 Print the block pattern from the CD onto foundation paper and trim close to the outside edges.

2 Cut the block into sections on the blue lines.

3 Complete all sections, leaving at least ¼" (6 mm) of fabric beyond the edges of each section. Press each section with spray starch. Trim each section ¼" (6 mm) past the pattern edges for the seam allowance.

4 Join A to F. Press seam toward F.

5 Join D to E. Press seam toward D.

6 Join AF to DE. Press seam open.

7 Join B to C. Press seam toward C.

8 Join ADEF to BC. Press seam toward ADEF.

9 Press block with spray starch.

10 Remove the paper from the back of the block in reverse sewing order for each section.

■ *Today's flat-screen TVs have none of the style* of an old-fashioned TV set. This is the perfect block to practice your fussy-cutting skills (page 21) to incorporate words, as I've done here, or pictures.

My Chair

Finished Size
8" × 8" (20.5 × 20.5 cm)

Fabric Needed
Woodgrain print fabric:
5" (12.5 cm) square for feet and arm

Green print fabric:
7" (18 cm) square for chair body

Violet fabric:
One fat eighth for background

ASSEMBLE THE BLOCK

1 Print the block pattern from the CD onto foundation paper and trim close to the outside edges.

2 Cut the block into sections on the blue lines.

3 Complete all sections, leaving at least ¼" (6 mm) of fabric beyond the edges of each section. Press each section with spray starch. Trim each section ¼" (6 mm) past the pattern edges for the seam allowance.

4 Join A to B. Press seam open.

5 Join C to AB. Press seam open.

6 Join F to ABC. Press seam open.

7 Join E to D. Press seam open.

8 Join ABCF to DE. Press seam open.

9 Press block with spray starch.

10 Remove the paper from the back of the block in reverse sewing order for each section.

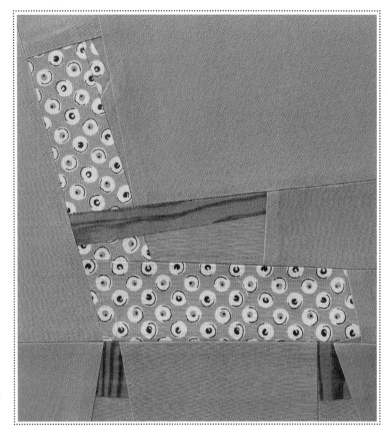

■ *If I owned this chair, it would be "my chair."*
It would be the place I would sit after a long stressful day at work, in the morning while drinking my latte, or while I'm crocheting or embroidering or talking on the phone....

Rotary Phone

■ *My husband and I have a red rotary phone* like this one. It isn't hooked up, but we keep it because we love it. We call it the "bat phone." We pretend that if it were to ring, we would answer it and need to make decisions of worldwide impact.

Finished Size
7" × 7" (18 × 18 cm)

Fabric Needed
Red fabric:
7" (18 cm) square for phone

Black print:
2" (5 cm) square for feet

Numeral print:
3" (7.5 cm) square for dial

Orange dot:
One fat sixteenth for background

Other Supplies
Embroidery floss (black used in the sample)

ASSEMBLE THE BLOCK

❶ Print the block pattern from the CD onto foundation paper and trim close to the outside edges.

❷ Cut the block into sections on the blue lines.

❸ Complete and trim all sections following the instructions on page 12.

❹ Join A to B. Press seam open.

❺ Join C to AB. Press seam toward C.

❻ Join D to E. Press seam open.

❼ Join F to DE. Press seam toward F.

❽ Join G to DEF. Press seam toward G.

❾ Join ABC to DEFG. Press seam open.

❿ Press block with spray starch.

⓫ Remove the paper from the back of the block in reverse sewing order for each section.

⓬ Print two copies of the reversed block pattern for embroidery and appliqué. Follow the instructions on page 26 to appliqué the dial onto the phone.

⓭ Following the instructions on page 24, transfer the cord to the pieced block and embroider with a back stitch.

tip
Instead of using a numeral print, you could stamp numbers on solid fabric for the appliquéd dial. See page 26 for instructions on stamping fabric.

Clawfoot Tub

Finished Size
12" × 12" (30.5 × 30.5 cm)

Fabric Needed

White fabric:
10" (25.5 cm) square for tub

Orange striped fabric:
3" (7.5 cm) square for towel

Dark gray fabric:
4" (10 cm) square for feet

Light gray fabric:
5" (12.5 cm) square for shower pole and head

Dark aqua fabric:
One fat quarter for background

Other Supplies
Embroidery floss (light blue used in the sample)

ASSEMBLE THE BLOCK

1 Print the block pattern from the CD onto foundation paper and trim close to the outside edges.

2 Cut the block into sections on the blue lines.

3 Complete and trim all sections following the instructions on page 12.

4 Join B to C. Press seam toward B.

5 Join D to BC. Press seam toward D.

6 Join A to BCD. Press seam open.

7 Join E to ABCD. Press seam toward E.

8 Join G to H. Press seam toward G.

9 Join F to GH. Press seam open.

10 Join I to FGH. Press seam toward I.

11 Join P to FGHI. Press seam open.

12 Join J to K. Press seam open.

13 Join L to JK. Press seam open.

14 Join M to N. Press seam open.

15 Join JKL to MN. Press seam open.

16 Join O to JKLMN. Press seam toward O.

Just thinking about a clawfoot tub makes me nostalgic. You can piece this block with or without the shower (as in the Clawfoot Bath Mat project on page 84).

17 Join JKLMNO to ABCDE. Press seam open.

18 Join ABCDEJKLMNO to FGHIP. Press seam open.

19 Press block with spray starch.

20 Remove the paper from the back of the block in reverse sewing order for each section.

21 Print two copies of the reversed block pattern for embroidery and appliqué. Following the instructions on page 24, transfer the water stream to the pieced block and embroider with a running stitch.

22 Follow the instructions on page 26 to appliqué the towel to the side of the tub.

Lamp

This lamp is simple and understated in style.
In construction, it has a few Y-seams that, although they add complexity, play nicely with the simplicity of the design. Make sure to read the section on Y-seams (page 23) before you start if you're unfamiliar with them.

Finished Size
10" × 12" (25.5 × 30.5 cm)

Fabric Needed
Dark pink fabric:
10" (25.5 cm) square for base

Blue floral fabric:
5" × 8" (12.5 × 20.5 cm) for shade

Dark gray fabric:
2" (5 cm) square for post and finial

Black-and-white print fabric:
3" × 8" (7.5 × 20.5 cm) for top and bottom edges of shade

Polka dot fabric:
One fat quarter for background

ASSEMBLE THE BLOCK

1 Print the block pattern from the CD onto foundation paper and trim close to the outside edges.

2 Cut the block into sections on the blue lines.

3 Complete all sections, leaving at least ¼" (6 mm) of fabric beyond the edges of each section. Press each section with spray starch. Trim each section ¼" (6mm) past the pattern edges for the seam allowance.

Note: When piecing sections C and D, do not sew past the edge of the pattern on the sewing lines with green dots. To prepare for the Y-seams between those sections, backstitch at the pattern edge instead.

4 Join B to C. Press seam open.

5 Join BC to D, following the instructions for Y-seams on page 23. Press seam toward BC.

6 Join E to BCD. Press seam toward E.

7 Join F to BCDE. Press seam toward F.

8 Join A to BCDEF. Press seam toward BCDEF.

9 Press block with spray starch.

10 Remove the paper from the back of the block in reverse sewing order for each section.

Footstool

The lines of this footstool are very traditional so I added a bit of funkiness with my fabric choices. This block would be a lovely addition to a pillow to go with the Trio of Pillows (page 78) in this chapter!

Finished Size
9" × 7" (23 × 18 cm)

Fabric Needed
Multicolored print:
9" × 3" (23 × 7.5 cm) for footstool cushion

Red fabric:
8" (20.5 cm) square for piping and feet

Red print:
8" × 4" (20.5 × 10 cm) for base

Gray fabric:
One fat eighth for background

ASSEMBLE THE BLOCK

1 Print the block pattern from the CD onto foundation paper and trim close to the outside edges.

2 Cut the block into sections on the blue lines.

3 Complete all sections, leaving at least ¼" (6 mm) of fabric beyond the edges of each section. Press each section with spray starch. Trim each section ¼" (6 mm) past the pattern edges for the seam allowance.

4 Join C to B. Press seam open.

5 Join D to BC. Press seam open.

6 Join A to BCD. Press seam toward A.

7 Join G to E. Press seam open.

8 Join H to EG. Press seam open.

9 Join F to EGH. Press seam open.

10 Join ABCD to EFGH. Press seam open.

11 Press block with spray starch.

12 Remove the paper from the back of the block in reverse sewing order for each section.

TRIO OF PILLOWS

Who says the pillow has to go on the couch? How about a couch on a pillow? Or a chair on a pillow? These tongue-in-cheek cushions will be conversation pieces as well as comfy additions to your living room. These practical covers have easy-zip closures and piping.

featured blocks
Couch (page 71), Telly (page 72), My Chair (page 73)

finished block sizes
Couch 16" × 6½" (40.5 × 16.5 cm)
Telly 10" × 12" (25.5 × 30.5 cm)
My Chair 15" × 15" (38 × 38 cm)

finished sizes
Couch Pillow 13½" × 23" (34.5 × 58.5 cm)
Telly Pillow 17" × 19" (43 × 48.5 cm)
Chair Pillow 22" (56 cm) square

Note: These block patterns have been resized for the pillows. Be sure to use the larger project patterns on the CD when constructing the pillows.

Fabric for Couch Pillow

Natural linen fabric:
- ½ yd (45.5 cm) for background
  — Cut 3 strips, 3" (7.5 cm) × width of fabric
  — Use the remainder for piecing the block

Orange plaid, off-white, and floral print fabrics:
- 15" (38 cm) square each for cushions and couch frame

Woodgrain fabric:
- 5" (12.5 cm) square for couch feet

Text print:
- ⅛ yd (11.5 cm) for block border
  — Cut 2 strips, 1½" (3.8 cm) × width of fabric

Coordinating scraps:
- ½ yd (45.5 cm) total for pillow back

Other Supplies for Couch Pillow
- Couch Pillow block pattern (on CD)
- 85" (216 cm) of prepared piping
- 18" (45.5 cm) zipper
- 14" × 23" (35.5 × 58.5 cm) pillow form

Fabric for Chair Pillow

Cream linen:
- ⅔ yd (61 cm) for background
  — Cut 4 rectangles, 3" × 24" (7.5 × 61 cm)
  — Use the remainder for piecing the block

Floral print:
- One fat quarter for chair

Dark gray print:
- 15" (38 cm) square for arm and legs

Text-print fabric:
- ⅛ yd (11.5 cm) for block border
  — Cut 2 strips, 1½" (3.8 cm) × width of fabric

Coordinating scraps:
- ⅔ yd (61 cm) total for back

Other Supplies for Chair Pillow
- My Chair Pillow block pattern (on CD)
- 100" (254 cm) of prepared piping
- 18" (45.5 cm) zipper
- 22" (56 cm) square pillow form

Fabric for Telly Pillow

Natural linen fabric:
- ½ yard (45.5 cm) for background
  — Cut 2 strips 3" (7.5 cm) × width of fabric
  — Use the remainder for piecing the block

Aqua fabric:
- One fat quarter for TV cabinet

Multicolored print fabric:
- 7" (18 cm) square for TV screen

Dark gray fabric:
- 10" (25.5 cm) square for legs

Text print:
- ⅛ yd (11.5 cm) for block border
  — Cut 2 strips 1½" (3.8 cm) × width of fabric

Coordinating scraps:
- ½ yd (45.5 cm) total for back

Other Supplies for Telly Pillow
- Telly Pillow block pattern (on CD)
- 85" (216 cm) of prepared piping
- 14" (35.5 cm) zipper
- 17" × 19" (43 × 48.5 cm) pillow form

Tools
Zipper foot

DIRECTIONS

1. Because these blocks are oversized, print each one in sections and tape them together, then proceed with piecing, following the instructions on page 71 for the Couch, page 72 for the Telly, and page 73 for My Chair.

2. Sew a strip of text print to one side of the pieced block. Trim the strip even with the block edges and press it outward. Sew a strip to the opposite side of the block, using the remainder of the same fabric strip. Repeat the sewing, trimming, and pressing to add borders to the top and bottom edges of the block.

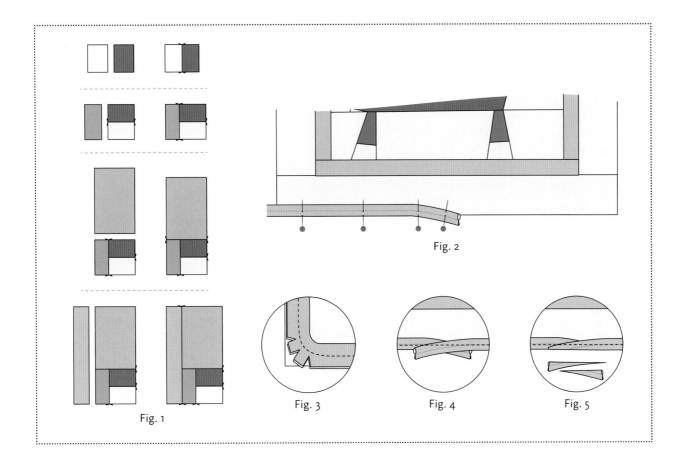

Fig. 2

Fig. 3

Fig. 4

Fig. 5

Fig. 1

3 Using the 3" (7.5 cm) × width of fabric linen strips (for the chair pillow, the 3" × 24" [7.5 × 61 cm] rectangles), repeat Step 2 to add a border to the assembled unit.

4 Using improvisational piecing techniques, piece a pillow back from scraps of pillow fabrics at least 1" (2.5 cm) larger on all sides than the pillow front **(fig. 1)**.

5 Trim the back so it is the same size as the front.

6 Align the raw edge of the piping with the raw edge of the pillow front and pin, starting at the center bottom. Curve the piping ends off the pillow raw edge and pin **(fig. 2)**. Using a zipper foot, sew the piping to the right side of the pillow front, stitching close to the piping cord.

7 As you sew around the corners, clip the piping seam allowances in three places to ease the piping around the corner **(fig. 3)**.

8 When you have sewn the piping all the way around the pillow front, overlap the end of the piping with the beginning; curve it off the pillow raw edge as you did at the beginning and finish stitching, sewing across the overlap. Trim the excess piping **(figs. 4 and 5)**.

9 Place the pillow back on the front, right sides together. To prepare for the zipper insertion, pin the lower edges together. Mark each side of the bottom seam 1" (2.5 cm) and 3½" (9 cm) from the side edges. Sew between each pair of marks, using the zipper foot. Backstitch at the beginning and end of each seam and sew very close to the piping cord.

Note: Leaving the 1" (2.5 cm) gap at the sides keeps the piping free at the corners.

tip
If you have the perfect fabric to use for piping, make your own! There are many tutorials online; just search for "how to make piping."

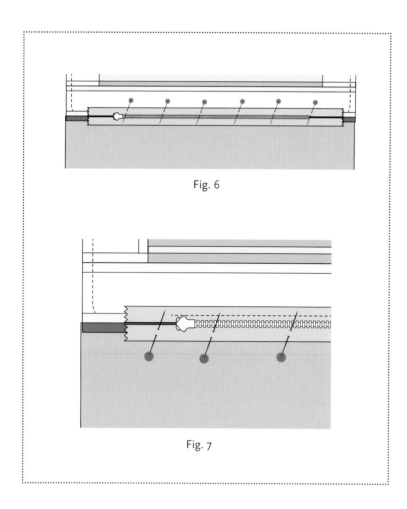

Fig. 6

Fig. 7

10 Open the pillow front and back. With the pillow wrong side up, place the closed zipper right side down on top of the pillow front and piping, with the zipper pull to the left. The zipper will extend into the seams at each end. Pin the zipper to the pillow front and use the zipper foot to sew the zipper to the pillow front, stitching close to the zipper teeth as they lie on top of the piping. The edges of the zipper tape and piping will not align (**fig. 6**).

11 Repeat Step 10 to sew the other side of the zipper to the pillow back, ignoring references to the piping (**fig. 7**).

12 Unzip the zipper halfway. Pin the pillow front and back, right sides together, and sew around the pillow close to the piping cord, starting and ending at the stitching from Step 9.

13 Turn the pillow cover right side out and insert the pillow form.

tip

Whenever possible, I use a pillow form slightly larger than the finished cover will be so that the pillow plumps out nicely. Therefore, the pillow forms for this project don't necessarily have to be the exact dimensions given here, as long as they are the correct shape (square or rectangle). Pillow forms may be up to an inch or two larger than the finished project dimensions. Alternatively, you can easily make your own pillow form with muslin and fiberfill stuffing. Simply cut two pieces of muslin measuring 2" (5 cm) larger in each dimension than the desired finished dimensions of the cover (this allows for ½" [1.3 cm] seam allowances and will give you a form that will plump out the cover). Then just sew, turn, fill, and stitch the gap closed—done!

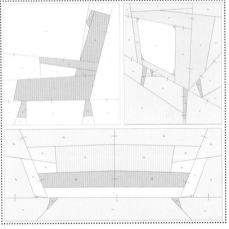

See the CD for the full-size block patterns.

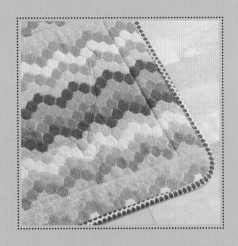

CLAWFOOT BATH MAT

Most of the bath mats I use in my home are handmade. The construction is pretty simple, and the mats have survived many washings. If you come across a fabulous bath towel, purchase it and use it to back a bath mat you make yourself!

featured block
Clawfoot Tub (page 75)

finished block size
22" × 14" (56 × 35.5 cm)

finished size
27½" × 19½" (70 × 49.5 cm)

Note: This block pattern has been resized and slightly redesigned for the bath mat. Be sure to use the larger project pattern on the CD when constructing the mat.

Fabric

Floral print:
- ½ yd (45.5 cm) for background of tub block

Red fabric:
- 10" (25.5 cm) square for tub feet

White fabric:
- 15" (38 cm) square for tub body

Red polka dot fabric:
- 4" × 15" (10 × 38 cm) for tub rim

Diagonal plaid print:
- ¼ yd (23 cm) for border

Terry cloth:
- ¾ yd (68.5 cm) (or large towel) for backing

White flannel:
- ¾ yd (68.5 cm) for lining

Large red polka dot fabric:
- ¼ yd (23 cm) for binding

Other Supplies
- Clawfoot Bath Mat block pattern (on CD)

Tools
- Walking foot
- Binding tool (optional, but helpful); see binding instructions on page 29

CUT THE FABRIC

From the diagonal plaid print, cut:

- ▶ 2 border strips, 3" (7.5 cm) × width of fabric

From the terry cloth, cut:

- ▶ 1 backing rectangle, 30" × 22" (76 × 56 cm)

From the white flannel, cut:

- ▶ 1 lining rectangle, 30" × 22" (76 × 56 cm)

From the large red dot, cut:

- ▶ 3 binding strips, 2½" (6.5 cm) × width of fabric

DIRECTIONS

1. Because the Clawfoot Tub bath mat block is oversized, print it in sections and tape them together, then proceed with piecing.

2. Trim the block pattern close to the outer edges. Cut the block into sections on the blue lines.

3. Complete all sections, leaving at least ¼" (6 mm) of fabric beyond the edges of each section. Press each section with spray starch. Trim each section ¼" (6 mm) past the pattern edges for the seam allowance.

4. Join B to C. Press toward C.

5. Join D to BC. Press seam open.

6. Join A to BCD. Press seam open.

7. Join E to ABCD. Press seam open.

8. Join K to ABCDE. Press seam open.

9. Join G to H. Press seam toward G.

10. Join F to GH. Press seam open.

11. Join I to FGH. Press seam open.

12. Join J to FGHI. Press seam toward FGHI.

13 Join ABCDEK to FGHIJ. Press seam open.

14 Press block with spray starch.

15 Remove the paper from the back of the block in reverse sewing order for each section.

16 Sew a 3" (7.5 cm) strip of the plaid print to one side of the pieced block. Trim the strip even with the block edges and press it outward. Sew a strip to the opposite side of the block, using the remainder of the same fabric strip. Repeat the sewing, trimming, and pressing to add borders to the top and bottom edges of the block.

17 Round the bath mat corners by tracing around a cup or bowl with a chalk pencil, then cut along the traced line.

18 Layer the towel, right side down; flannel; and pieced bath mat front, right side up. Baste with pins.

19 Quilt the layers by stitching in the ditch around the tub block, using a walking foot if desired. Echo quilt ⅛" (3 mm) outside the entire tub and inside the white tub area.

20 Trim the toweling and flannel to match the bath mat front.

21 Baste ⅛" (3 mm) from the edge of the mat.

22 Bind the mat with the red polka dot strips, using a walking foot and following the instructions on page 29.

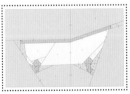

See the CD for the full-size block pattern.

CHAPTER 6

Create & Organize

I hope you find the creativity-inspired blocks and useful projects in this chapter fresh and fun. I thrive in an organized environment, and if my craft room or any area of my home is in disarray I feel stifled, which compels me to put everything back in its place to get the creative juices flowing.

Block Key

22 Stack of Books

23 Sewing Machine

24 Stapler

25 Paper Clip

Full-size patterns are included on the CD.

Stack of Books

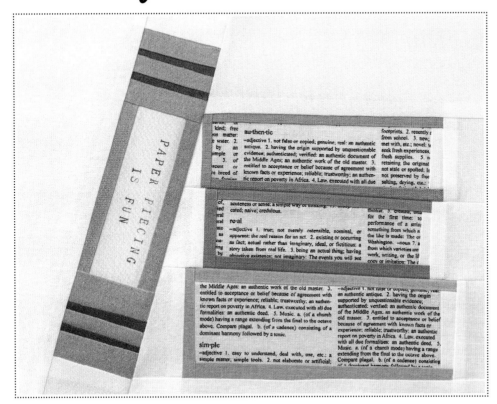

■ *This assortment of books* is a reminder that although paper piecing can be intense at times, it is indeed fun!

Finished Size
10" × 10" (25.5 × 25.5 cm)

Fabric Needed

Orange, pink, and aqua fabrics:
3" × 9" (7.5 × 23 cm) of each for stacked book covers

Text-print fabric:
9" (23 cm) square for pages

Green fabric:
7" (18 cm) square for vertical book cover

Off-white fabric:
3" × 6" (7.5 × 15 cm) for vertical book title area

Dark blue fabric:
3" × 5" (7.5 × 12.5 cm) for vertical book accents

White fabric:
One fat sixteenth for background

Other Supplies
Letter stamps
Permanent fabric ink

ASSEMBLE THE BLOCK

1 Print the block pattern from the CD onto foundation paper and trim close to the outside edges.

2 Cut the block into sections on the blue lines.

3 Following the stamping instructions on page 26, stamp "Paper Piecing Is Fun" on the fabric for the vertical book's title area.

4 Complete all sections, leaving at least ¼" (6 mm) of fabric beyond the edges of each section. Press each section with spray starch. Trim each section ¼" (6 mm) past the pattern edges for the seam allowance.

5 Join B to C. Press seam open.

6 Join D to BC. Press seam open.

7 Join A to BCD. Press seam toward A.

8 Press block with spray starch.

9 Remove the paper from the back of the block in reverse sewing order for each section.

Sewing Machine

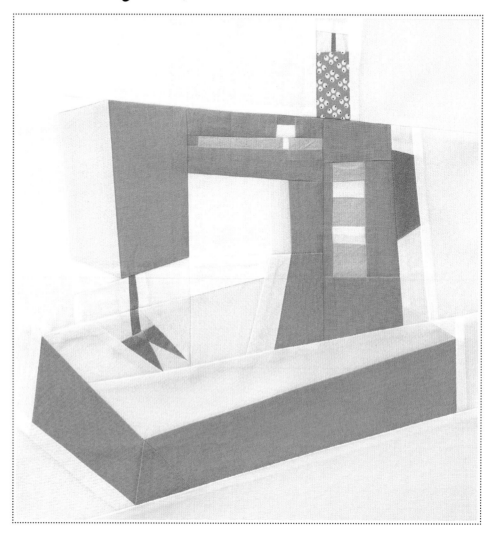

■ *Sewing is a huge part of my life.* This block celebrates my love for sewing with what I consider the quintessential sewing machine!

Finished Size
15" × 15" (38 × 38 cm)

Fabric Needed

Aqua fabric:
One fat quarter for machine body

Off-white fabric:
One fat eighth for machine body

Dark gray fabric:
5" (12.5 cm) square for presser foot, wheel, and spool holder

Light gray fabric:
7" (18 cm) square for machine details

Orange print fabric:
4" (10 cm) square for thread spool

White fabric:
⅓ yd (30.5 cm) for background and machine details

ASSEMBLE THE BLOCK

1 Print the block pattern from the CD onto foundation paper and trim close to the outside edges.

2 Cut the block into sections on the blue lines.

3 Complete all sections, leaving at least ¼" (6 mm) of fabric beyond the edges of each section. Press each section with spray starch. Trim each section ¼" (6 mm) past the pattern edges for the seam allowance.

4 Join J to K. Press seam toward K.

5 Join L to JK. Press seam toward L.

6 Join M to JKL. Press toward M.

7 Join I to H. Press toward H.

8 Join HI to N. Press toward HI.

9 Join JKLM to HIN. Press toward HIN.

10 Join B to C. Press toward C.

11 Join A to BC. Press toward BC.

12 Join D to E. Press toward E.

13 Join ABC to DE. Press seam open.

14 Join F to G. Press seam open.

15 Join FG to ABCDE. Press seam toward ABCDE.

16 Join ABCDEFG to HIJKLMN. Press seam open.

17 Join O to ABCDEFGHIJKLMN. Press seam toward O.

18 Join P to ABCDEFGHIJKLMNO. Press seam open.

19 Join Q to ABCDEFGHIJKLMNOP. Press seam open.

20 Join R to ABCDEFGHIJKLMNOPQ. Press seam open.

21 Press block with spray starch.

22 Remove the paper from the back of the block in reverse sewing order for each section.

Use the Sewing Machine block to create an organizer for all your notions (page 100).

Stapler

■ *I have several staplers around* my house, but none are as fair as this one. This block would be adorable framed above a desk as a reminder to keep things organized!

Finished Size
10" × 6" (25.5 × 15 cm)

Fabric Needed
Floral fabric:
7" (18 cm) square for stapler body

Red checked fabric:
3" (7.5 cm) square for details

White fabric:
12" (30.5 cm) square for background

ASSEMBLE THE BLOCK

1 Print the block pattern from the CD onto foundation paper and trim close to the outside edges.

2 Cut the block into sections on the blue lines.

3 Complete all sections, leaving at least ¼" (6 mm) of fabric beyond the edges of each section. Press each section with spray starch. Trim each section ¼" (6 mm) past the pattern edges for the seam allowance.

4 Join B to C. Press seam toward B.

5 Join D to E. Press seam open.

6 Join BC to DE. Press seam open.

7 Join A to BCDE. Press seam open.

8 Press block with spray starch.

9 Remove the paper from the back of the block in reverse sewing order for each section.

Paper Clip

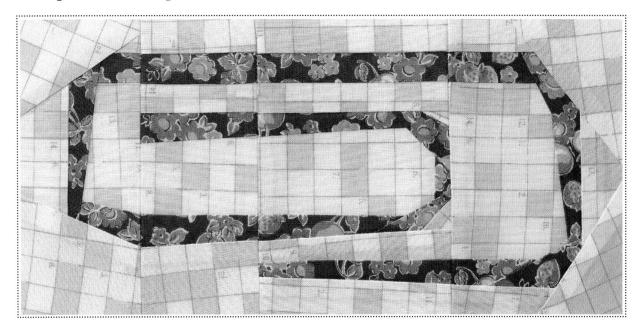

Even an object as humble as a paper clip can provide inspiration for a block design or even an entire project (page 94). Try it in a stripe, polka dot, or other favorite fabric.

Finished Size
5½" × 10¼" (14 × 26 cm)

Fabric Needed
Floral fabric:
10" (25.5 cm) square for paper clip

Gray-and-white print fabric:
One fat eighth for background

ASSEMBLE THE BLOCK

1 Print the block pattern from the CD onto foundation paper and trim close to the outside edges.

2 Cut the block into sections on the blue lines.

3 Complete all sections, leaving at least ¼" (6 mm) of fabric beyond the edges of each section. Press each section with spray starch. Trim each section ¼" (6 mm) past the pattern edges for the seam allowance.

4 Join A to B. Press seam open.

5 Join C to AB. Press seam open.

6 Join D to ABC. Press seam open.

7 Press block with spray starch.

8 Remove the paper from the back of the block in reverse sewing order for each section.

TABLET TOTE

This tote is perfectly sized for your tablet computer to fit snugly inside. The versatile strap can be arranged from one side to the other or clipped to the D-ring on the same side to form a loop. I try to buy from smaller businesses when I can, and I found the hardware for the tote on Etsy.

featured block
Paper Clip (page 93)

finished block size
6" × 3½" (15 × 9 cm)

finished size
Body 9¾" × 8" (25 × 20.5 cm)

Note: The block pattern has been resized for the Tablet Tote. Be sure to use the smaller project pattern on the CD when constructing the project.

Fabric

- ¼ yd (23 cm) of pink fabric for paper clip and strap
- One fat eighth of off-white fabric for block background
- One fat quarter of diagonal plaid print for border and tote back
- One fat quarter of black-and-white print for lining
- ⅛ yd (11.5 cm) of text print for inner border
- 4" × 5¼" (10 × 13.5 cm) scrap of multicolored print for closure tab

Other Supplies

- Paper Clip Tablet Tote block pattern (on CD)
- 16" × 18" (40.5 × 45.5 cm) piece of batting
- One sew-in magnetic closure, ¾" (2 cm) diameter
- One ½" (1.3 cm) D-ring
- One ½" (1.3 cm) swivel hook

CUT THE FABRIC

From the pink fabric, cut:

▸ 1 strap and loop strip, 2" × 20" (5 × 51 cm)

▸ Reserve the remaining fabric for piecing the block

From the lining fabric, cut:

▸ 1 lining rectangle, 10¼" × 16½" (26 × 42 cm)

▸ 1 closure tab rectangle, 4" × 5¼" (10 × 13.5 cm)

From the text print, cut:

▸ 2 inner borders, 1" × 4" (2.5 × 10 cm)

▸ 2 inner borders, 1" × 7½" (2.5 × 19 cm)

From the plaid print, cut:

▸ 1 back and bottom, 10" × 10¼" (25.5 × 26 cm)

▸ 2 outer borders, 1⅞" × 7" (4.7 × 18 cm)

▸ 1 outer border, 2½" × 7½" (6.5 × 19 cm)

From the multicolor print, cut:

▸ 1 closure tab, 4" × 5¼" (10 × 13.5 cm)

From the batting, cut:

▸ 1 tote body, 12" × 18" (30.5 × 45.5 cm)

▸ 1 closure tab, 4" × 5¼" (10 × 13.5 cm)

DIRECTIONS

❶ Piece the Paper Clip block following the instructions on page 93.

❷ Sew the 1" × 4" (2.5 × 10 cm) text-print rectangles to the short ends of the pieced block. Add the 1" × 7½" (2.5 × 19 cm) rectangles to the top and bottom. Stitch the 2½" × 7½" (6.5 × 19 cm) plaid rectangle to the top of the assembled unit and add the 1⅞" × 7" (4.7 × 18 cm) plaid rectangles to the sides. Sew the assembled section to the 10" × 10¼" (25.5 × 26 cm) plaid rectangle to complete the tote's outer body.

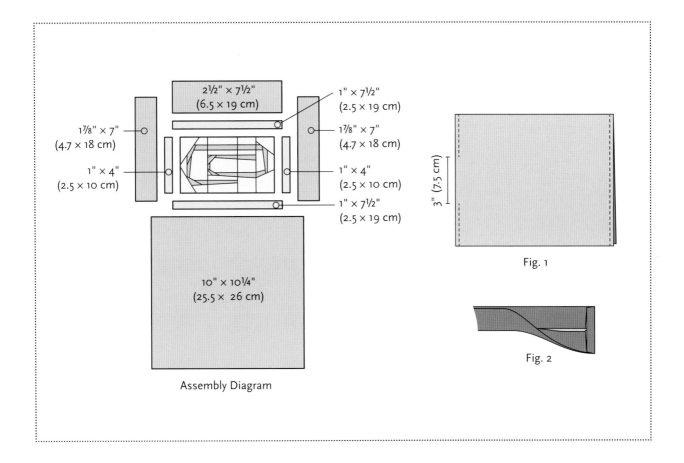

Assembly Diagram

2½" × 7½"
(6.5 × 19 cm)

1" × 7½"
(2.5 × 19 cm)

1⅞" × 7"
(4.7 × 18 cm)

1⅞" × 7"
(4.7 × 18 cm)

1" × 4"
(2.5 × 10 cm)

1" × 4"
(2.5 × 10 cm)

1" × 7½"
(2.5 × 19 cm)

10" × 10¼"
(25.5 × 26 cm)

3" (7.5 cm)

Fig. 1

Fig. 2

3 Center the outer body, right side up, on the large batting rectangle. Baste with pins and echo quilt ⅛" (3 mm) outside the paper clip, block, and inner border. Quilt randomly spaced lines on the rest of the bag to resemble a plaid.

4 Center and sew one of the magnetic closures to the batting side of the bag 1¼" (3.2 cm) from the top edge.

Note: Plan carefully to disguise the stitches around the magnetic closure within the lines of quilting.

5 Fold the outer body in half, right sides together, and stitch the side seams. Clip the bottom corners slightly to remove bulk and turn the bag right side out.

6 Fold the lining in half with right sides together and stitch the side seams, leaving a 3" (7.5 cm) gap near the center of one side. Backstitch the beginning and end of each seam, and on each side of the gap **(fig. 1)**.

7 Press the 2" × 20" (5 × 51 cm) strap and loop strip in half lengthwise with wrong sides together. Open the fold and press both long edges to meet the center crease. Refold along the original crease and press once more, enclosing the long raw edges.

8 Cut two 1¾" (4.5 cm) loops and one 15" (38 cm) strap from the prepared strip.

9 Temporarily unfold the strap and press ¼" (6 mm) to the wrong side on each short end. Refold and press again **(fig. 2)**.

10 Edgestitch all four edges of the strap and both long edges of each loop.

11 Fold one loop in half around the D-ring, matching the raw edges. Center the loop over the left side seam on the outside of the bag body, aligning the raw edges, and baste (**fig. 3**).

12 Fold the second loop in half, matching the raw edges. Center the loop over the right side seam on the outside of the bag body, aligning the raw edges, and baste.

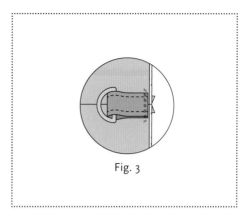

Fig. 3

13 Place the outside of the bag inside the lining, right sides together, and sew the top edge.

14 Turn the bag right side out through the gap in the lining side seam, and then hand or machine stitch the lining closed.

15 Press the top of the bag flat and topstitch ¼" (6 mm) from the edge.

16 Thread one end of the strap through the D-ring from the outside. Fold 1½" (3.8 cm) of the strap to the wrong side and sew the strap ends together, enclosing the D-ring.

17 Repeat Step 16 to attach the swivel hook to the other end of the strap.

18 Center the second half of the magnetic closure on the wrong side of the lining for the tab closure, 1¼" (3.2 cm) above one short end, and sew into place.

Note: Before sewing, make sure the magnets are placed correctly so they attract each other when the tote is closed.

19 Layer the tab lining, right side up; outer fabric, right side down; and batting. Round the two corners near the magnetic closure and trim.

20 Sew the tab along all four edges, leaving a 2" (5 cm) opening in the short edge without the magnet. Turn and press, turning the raw edges to the inside along the gap. Topstitch ¼" (6 mm) from the edges.

21 Fasten the magnetic closure and fold the other end of the tab to the back of the bag, centering it. Unfasten the magnetic closure and pin the back end of the tab to the back of the tote. Stitch along the bottom edge of the tab, sewing over the topstitching. Stitch again, ½" (1.3 cm), above the end of the tab.

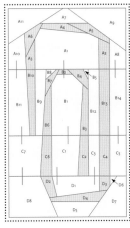

See the CD for the full-size block pattern.

SEWING ORGANIZER

This colorful organizer is a cute and practical way to keep those items you use most often in your sewing area at your fingertips. If you have favorite tools that are different than the ones marked on this organizer, stitch those names on the pockets instead to customize the organizer to fit your needs.

featured block
Sewing Machine (page 90)

finished size
17½" × 27½" (44.5 × 70 cm)

Notes

▶ If your machine has a "triple straight stitch" (with a sewing pattern of forward, backward, and then forward again for each stitch), use it where indicated in the pattern. If not, use a heavy topstitching thread or embroider by hand using 3 strands of floss.

▶ When embroidering the words onto the pockets and plaque, use a sashiko stitch. This traditional Japanese version of a running stitch features stitches that are longer than the spaces in between, with the goal being a very uniform appearance and consistent stitch length.

Fabric

- Fabrics for Sewing Machine block (page 90)
- ½ yd (45.5 cm) of natural linen fabric for background and pockets
- ⅞ yd (80 cm) of multicolor print fabric for backing and pocket lining
- ½ yd (45.5 cm) of orange print fabric for binding, tabs, and scissors strip

Other Supplies

- 20" × 30" (51 × 76 cm) piece of batting
- 6-strand embroidery floss (black used in the sample) and needle
- Sewing Machine block pattern (on CD)
- Word embroidery patterns (page 133)

CUT THE FABRIC

From the linen, cut:

- ▶ 2 side borders, 1½" × 15½" (3.8 × 39.5 cm)
- ▶ 1 top border, 2¼" × 17½" (5.5 × 44.5 cm)
- ▶ 1 lower front, 11" × 17½" (28 × 44.5 cm)
- ▶ 1 sectioned pocket, 10" × 5½" (25.5 × 14 cm)
- ▶ 1 ruler pocket, 12" × 2½" (30.5 × 6.5 cm)
- ▶ 1 scissors plaque, 2½" × 5" (6.5 × 12.5 cm)

From the print fabric, cut:

- ▶ 1 backing rectangle, 20" × 30" (51 × 76 cm)
- ▶ 1 sectioned pocket, 10" × 5½" (25.5 × 14 cm)
- ▶ 1 ruler pocket, 12" × 2½" (30.5 × 6.5 cm)
- ▶ 1 scissors plaque, 2½" × 5" (6.5 × 12.5 cm)

From the orange print, cut:

- ▶ 5 strips, 2½" (6.5 cm) × width of fabric, for binding, tabs, and scissors strip

DIRECTIONS

1 Piece the Sewing Machine block (page 90).

2 Sew a linen side border to each side of the block.

3 Sew a top border to the upper edge of the assembled unit.

4 Sew the lower front rectangle to the bottom of the assembled unit.

5 Layer the backing, right side down; batting; and organizer front, right side up. Baste with pins.

6 Echo quilt ⅛" (3 mm) outside the sewing machine by hand with embroidery floss.

7 Trim the batting and backing to match the front of the organizer. Bind the organizer with the 2½" (6.5 cm) wide orange print strips, following the instructions on page 29. Reserve the leftover strip length.

8 Triple stitch (see note on page 101) ⅛" (3 mm) outside the sewing machine block.

9 With right sides together, sew the linen and lining pocket and plaque pieces together, leaving a 2" (5 cm) gap along one long edge of each for turning.

10 Trim the corners diagonally to reduce bulk. Turn the pockets and plaque right side out, folding the seam allowances to the wrong side along the gaps, and press. Use a thin bead of water-soluble glue to tack the opening closed.

11 Embroider the words on the pockets as shown, using a sashiko stitch (see note on page 101).

12 Use the triple stitch to edgestitch the scissors plaque onto the organizer, ⅞" (2.2 cm) below the sewing machine block and 1¼" (3.2 cm) from the left edge.

13 Use the triple stitch to edgestitch the ruler pocket onto the organizer, 1⅛" (2.9 cm) above the bottom edge and 3" (7.5 cm) from the right edge. Leave the short end on the right open.

14 Position the sectioned pocket on the organizer, 2" (5 cm) below the sewing machine block and 1⅛" (2.9 cm) from the right raw edge. Be sure the glued opening is along the bottom edge so it will be secured by the edgestitching. Use the triple stitch to edgestitch the side and lower edges of the pocket.

15 Triple stitch 2" (5 cm) from the left edge of the sectioned pocket to divide the pocket, creating the seam ripper section. Triple stitch 2½" (6.5 cm) from the right edge of the pocket to create the markers section.

16 To create the scissors strip, cut a 5" (12.5 cm) length from the leftover binding strip. Fold it in half lengthwise, with wrong sides together, and press. Open the fold and press both long edges in to meet at the center

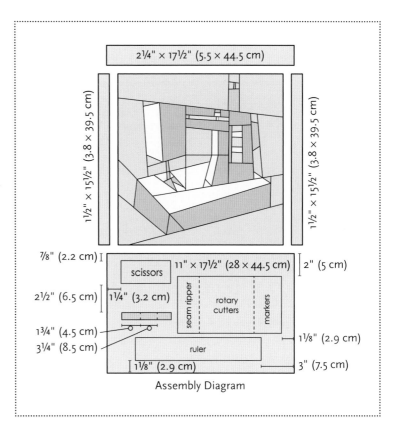

2¼" × 17½" (5.5 × 44.5 cm)

1½" × 15½" (3.8 × 39.5 cm)

1½" × 15½" (3.8 × 39.5 cm)

⅞" (2.2 cm)

2½" (6.5 cm)   1¼" (3.2 cm)

1¾" (4.5 cm)
3¼" (8.5 cm)

scissors

11" × 17½" (28 × 44.5 cm)   2" (5 cm)

seam ripper   rotary cutters   markers

1⅛" (2.9 cm)

ruler

1⅛" (2.9 cm)   3" (7.5 cm)

Assembly Diagram

crease. Press ¼" (6 mm) to the wrong side on each short end. Refold along the original crease and press once more. Edgestitch both long edges with the triple stitch.

17 Position the scissors strip on the organizer, 2½" (6.5 cm) below the scissor plaque and 1¼" (3.2 cm) from the left raw edge. Triple stitch from top to bottom across the strip, ⅛" (3 mm) from each end. Stitch again 1¾" (4.5 cm) and 3¼" (8.5 cm) from the left edge to divide the strip into three sections.

18 To make the hanging tabs, cut two 10" (25.5 cm) lengths from the leftover binding strip. Press each as directed in Step 16. Edgestitch all four edges of each tab.

19 Fold the hanging tabs in half. Position each one along the top edge of the organizer, 1" (2.5 cm) from the side edges, with the fold just below the binding. Stitch in the ditch of the binding seam to attach the fold of each hanging tab to the organizer. Tie the ends of each tab into a knot.

tip

If your favorite ruler is wider than 1" (2.5 cm), adjust the ruler pocket to fit your ruler.

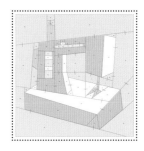

See the CD for the full-size block pattern.

CHAPTER 7

Playtime

This is one of my very favorite chapters, maybe because the childlike designs—from whimsical animals to a few toys I fondly remember playing with as a child—appeal to my playful side.

Block Key

26 Allie-Gator

27 Lion

28 Viewfinder Toy

29 Grown-up Paper Doll Dress

30 Bulldozer

31 Car Truck

32 Giraffe

33 Popper Push Toy

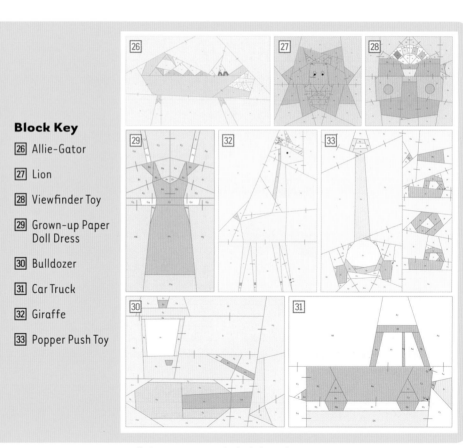

Full-size patterns are included on the CD.

Allie-Gator

Finished Size
18" × 11" (45.5 × 28 cm)

Fabric Needed
Green print:
15" (38 cm) square for Allie-Gator body

Medium blue fabric:
10" (25.5 cm) square for spines

White fabric:
6" (15 cm) square eye centers and teeth

Dark gray fabric:
3" (7.5 cm) square for eye outline

Light blue fabric:
⅓ yd (30.5 cm) for background

ASSEMBLE THE BLOCK

1 Print the block pattern from the CD onto foundation paper and trim close to the outside edges.

2 Cut the block into sections on the blue lines.

3 Complete all sections, leaving at least ¼" (6 mm) of fabric beyond the edges of each section. Press each section with spray starch.

Trim each section ¼" (6 mm) past the pattern edges for the seam allowance.

4 Join B to C. Press seam toward C.

5 Join A to BC. Press seam toward A.

6 Join D to E. Press toward E.

7 Join DE to ABC. Press toward ABC.

8 Join L to ABCDE. Press seam toward L.

9 Join F to G. Press seam toward F.

10 Join H to FG. Press seam toward H.

11 Join J to ABCDEL. Press seam toward J.

12 Join K to ABCDEJL. Press seam toward K.

13 Join FGH to ABCDEJKL. Press seam toward ABCDEJKL.

14 Join I to ABCDEFGHJKL. Press seam toward I.

15 Join M to N. Press seam toward M.

16 Join MN to ABCDEFGHIJKL. Press seam toward ABCDEFGHIJKL.

17 Press block with spray starch.

18 Remove the paper from the back of the block in reverse sewing order for each section.

Those teeth sure do look sharp, but have no fear. This reptile is as friendly as they come.

Lion

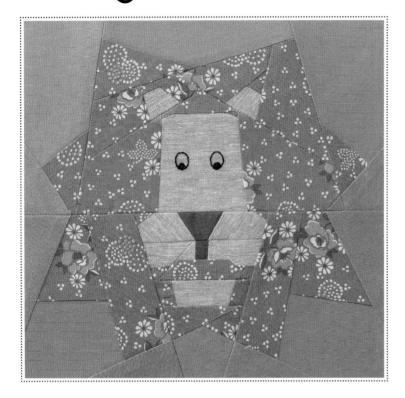

■ *This lion reminds me of the Cowardly Lion* from *The Wizard of Oz*. He's the king of the jungle but scared of mice. I think this harmless fellow would also look great with a polka dot mane.

Finished Size
10" × 10" (25.5 × 25.5 cm)

Fabric Needed
Dark pink print:
12" (30.5 cm) square for mane

Beige fabric:
7" (18 cm) square for face

Dark gray fabric:
4" (10 cm) square for nose

Green fabric:
One fat quarter for background

Other Materials
Embroidery floss (black used in the sample)

ASSEMBLE THE BLOCK

❶ Print the block pattern from the CD onto foundation paper and trim close to the outside edges.

❷ Cut the block into sections on the blue lines.

❸ Complete all sections, leaving at least ¼" (6 mm) of fabric beyond the edges of each section. Press each section with spray starch. Trim each section ¼" (6 mm) past the pattern edges for the seam allowance.

❹ Join A to C. Press seam open.

❺ Join AC to B. Press seam open.

❻ Join D to ABC. Press seam open.

❼ Join E to ABCD. Press seam open.

❽ Join F to ABCDE. Press seam open.

❾ Join H to J. Press seam toward H.

❿ Join I to HJ. Press seam toward HJ.

⓫ Join G to HIJ. Press seam toward G.

⓬ Join K to GHIJ. Press seam toward GHIJ.

⓭ Join L to GHIJK. Press seam toward L.

⓮ Join M to GHIJKL. Press seam toward M.

⓯ Join N to GHIJKLM. Press seam toward N.

⓰ Join ABCDEF to GHIJKLMN.

⓱ Press block with spray starch.

⓲ Remove the paper from the back of the block in reverse sewing order for each section.

⓳ Print a second copy of the block pattern for embroidery. Following the embroidery instructions on page 24, use embroidery floss to embroider the eyes (6 strands were used in the sample for thickness). Use a satin stitch for the pupils and backstitch for the outlines.

Viewfinder Joy

Finished Size
8" × 8" (20.5 × 20.5 cm)

Fabric Needed

Dark red fabric:
7" (18 cm) square for darker body area

Medium red fabric:
5" (12.5 cm) square for lighter body area

White fabric:
7" (18 cm) square for slide wheel

Dark gray fabric:
4" (10 cm) square for appliquéd eyeholes

Dark aqua fabric:
3" (7.5 cm) square for slide advancer

Off-white fabric:
2" (5 cm) square for body detail

Assorted prints:
Four 1½" (3.8 cm) pieces for fussy-cut images
(images must be less than ½" [1.3 cm] square)

Blue polka dot fabric:
One fat eighth for background

ASSEMBLE THE BLOCK

1 Print the block pattern from the CD onto foundation paper and trim close to the outside edges.

2 Cut the block into sections on the blue lines.

3 Complete and trim all sections following the instructions on page 12.

4 Join B to C. Press seam open.

5 Join D to E. Press seam open.

6 Join A to BC. Press toward A.

7 Join DE to ABC. Press toward ABC.

8 Join G to H. Press seam toward G.

9 Join I to J. Press seam toward J.

10 Join GH to IJ. Press seam open.

11 Join N to GHIJ. Press seam toward N.

12 Join L to GHIJN. Press seam toward L.

13 Join K to GHIJLN. Press seam toward K.

14 Join M to GHIJKLN. Press seam toward M.

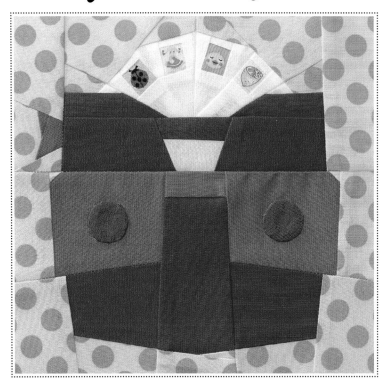

■ *Who didn't love those old viewfinder toys?*
You could sit on the floor with a stack of cardboard discs and click through colorful 3D images to your heart's content. It's the perfect block for tiny fussy-cut images from your favorite prints.

15 Join F to GHIJKLMN. Press seam toward F.

16 Join O to FGHIJKLMN. Press seam toward O.

17 Join P to FGHIJKLMNO. Press seam toward P.

18 Join ABCDE to FGHIJKLMNOP. Press seam open.

19 Press block with spray starch.

20 Remove the paper from the back of the block in reverse sewing order for each section.

21 Print a second copy of the block pattern for appliqué. Follow the appliqué instructions on page 26 to appliqué the eyeholes.

Grown-up Paper Doll Dress

Finished Size
4½" × 8" (11.5 × 20.5 cm)

Fabric Needed
Pink polka dot fabric:
9" (23 cm) square for dress

White fabric:
3" (7.5 cm) square for tabs

Light blue fabric:
One fat sixteenth for background

ASSEMBLE THE BLOCK

❶ Print the block pattern from the CD onto foundation paper and trim close to the outside edges.

❷ Cut the block into sections on the blue lines.

❸ Complete all sections, leaving at least ¼" (6 mm) of fabric beyond the edges of each section. Press each section with spray starch. Trim each section ¼" (6 mm) past the pattern edges for the seam allowance.

❹ Join A to B. Press seam open.

❺ Join C to AB. Press seam toward C.

❻ Join D to E. Press seam open.

❼ Join F to DE. Press seam toward F.

❽ Join ABC to DEF. Press seam open.

❾ Join G to H. Press seam open.

❿ Join ABCDEF to GH. Press seam open.

⓫ Press block with spray starch.

⓬ Remove the paper from the back of the block in reverse sewing order for each section.

I remember playing with paper dolls when I was a kid, but their clothes didn't look like this! This dress is totally devoid of ruffles, lace, and the typical high collar. I wouldn't mind wearing this little number myself.

Bulldozer

Finished Size
10" × 8" (25.5 × 20.5 cm)

Fabric Needed

Yellow fabric:
12" (30.5 cm) square for body and blade

White fabric:
3" (7.5 cm) square for window

Red fabric:
1" (2.5 cm) square flashing light

Black fabric:
5" (12.5 cm) square for blade connectors

Dark yellow fabric:
2" × 4" (5 × 10 cm) for roof

Dark gray fabric:
4" × 9" (10 × 23 cm) for track wheels

Light blue fabric:
One fat eighth for background

Other Materials
Embroidery floss (black used in the sample)

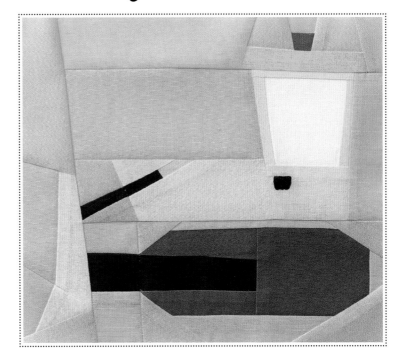

ASSEMBLE THE BLOCK

① Print the block pattern from the CD onto foundation paper and trim close to the outside edges.

② Cut the block into sections on the blue lines.

③ Complete and trim all sections following the instructions on page 12.

④ Join B to C. Press seam open.

⑤ Join D to BC. Press seam open.

⑥ Join A to BCD. Press seam open.

⑦ Join E to ABCD. Press seam toward E.

⑧ Join F to G. Press seam open.

⑨ Join ABCDE to FG. Press seam toward ABCDE.

I can think of so many uses for this block in your little guy's (or girl's) room. Stitch it into a seat cushion, a pillow top, or a soft play cube. Or, replace the clawfoot tub on the bath mat project (page 84) with an enlarged bulldozer pattern to make a sweet floor mat!

⑩ Join H to I. Press seam open.

⑪ Join HI to ABCDEFG. Press seam toward HI.

⑫ Press block with spray starch.

⑬ Remove the paper from the back of the block in reverse sewing order for each section.

⑭ Print a copy of the reversed block pattern for appliqué. Following the embroidery instructions on page 24, stitch the door handle. Use a satin stitch outlined with backstitch (6 strands of floss were used in the sample).

Car Truck

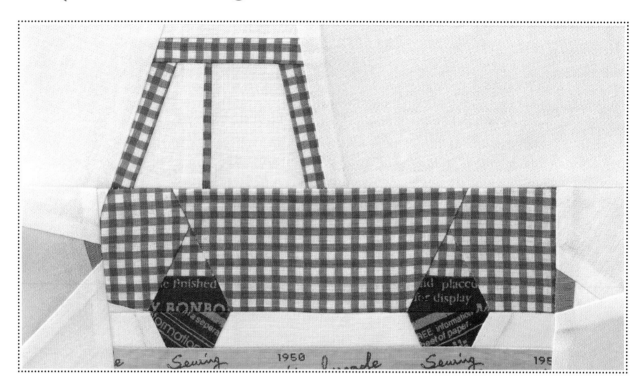

■ *Smaller than a truck, bigger than a car,* the car truck is at your service. It features a large bed ready to transport appliquéd balls from here to there.

Finished Size
9" × 7" (23 × 18 cm)

Fabric Needed

Dark gray print fabric:
4" (10 cm) square for tires

Light gray fabric:
2" (5 cm) square for bumper and headlight

Red-and-white checked fabric:
10" (25.5 cm) square for body

Yellow fabric:
3" (7.5 cm) square for light

Blue print fabric:
2" × 8" (5 × 20.5 cm) for road

White fabric:
One fat eighth for windows and background

ASSEMBLE THE BLOCK

1 Print the block pattern from the CD onto foundation paper and trim close to the outside edges.

2 Cut the block into sections on the blue lines.

3 Complete all sections, leaving at least ¼" (6 mm) of fabric beyond the edges of each section. Press each section with spray starch. Trim each section ¼" (6 mm) past the pattern edges for the seam allowance.

4 Join B to C. Press seam open.

5 Join D to BC. Press seam open.

6 Join E to BCD. Press seam toward E.

7 Join F to BCDE. Press seam toward F.

8 Join A to BCDEF. Press seam open.

9 Press block with spray starch.

10 Remove the paper from the back of the block in reverse sewing order for each section.

Finished Size
10" × 16" (25.5 × 40.5 cm)

Fabric Needed
Blue dotted fabric:
One fat eighth for giraffe body and legs

Light brown fabric:
5" (12.5 cm) square for ossicones ("horns"),
mane, and tail

Dark gray fabric:
4" (10 cm) square for feet

Yellow-green fabric:
One fat quarter for background

Other Materials
Embroidery floss (black used in the sample)

ASSEMBLE THE BLOCK

1 Print the block pattern from the CD onto foundation paper and trim close to the outside edges.

2 Cut the block into sections on the blue lines.

3 Complete and trim all sections following the instructions on page 12.

4 Join B to C. Press seam toward B.

5 Join A to BC. Press seam toward A.

6 Join D to ABC. Press seam toward D.

7 Join E to ABCD. Press seam toward E.

8 Join G to F. Press seam toward F.

9 Join H to FG. Press seam open.

10 Join FGH to ABCDE. Press seam open.

11 Join I to ABCDEFGH. Press seam toward I.

12 Join J to K. Press seam open.

13 Join L to M. Press seam open.

14 Join JK to LM. Press seam open.

15 Join JKLM to ABCDEFGHI. Press seam open.

16 Press block with spray starch.

17 Remove the paper from the back of the block in reverse sewing order for each section.

18 Backstitch (see page 24) the eye using 3 strands of floss.

Giraffe

■ *If giraffes are more your thing, replace the* Allie-Gator in the quilt project (page 114) with this sweet creature. Just enlarge the giraffe pattern and adjust the border sizes in the quilt.

Popper Push Toy

In my opinion, the popper push toy is one of the best toys ever invented! I remember the distinct "pop!" noise it made, so I included the word "pop!" in the design. If you prefer to piece only the toy, feel free to cut off the word part of the pattern and discard it.

Finished Size

10" × 12" (25.5 × 30.5 cm)

Fabric Needed

Scraps of orange print fabrics for letters

Blue polka dot fabric:

2" × 10" (5 × 25.5 cm) for handle

Red polka dot fabric:

2" (5 cm) square for pop top

Red checked fabric:

3" (7.5 cm) square for wheels

Aqua fabric:

3" (7.5 cm) square for toy base stripe

White fabric:

3" (7.5 cm) square for toy base

Light yellow fabric:

One fat sixteenth for background

ASSEMBLE THE BLOCK

1 Print the block pattern from the CD onto foundation paper and trim close to the outside edges.

2 Cut the block into sections on the blue lines.

3 Complete all sections, leaving at least ¼" (6 mm) of fabric beyond the edges of each section. Press each section with spray starch. Trim each section ¼" (6 mm) past the pattern edges for the seam allowance.

4 Join A to B. Press seam toward B.

5 Join C to AB. Press seam open.

6 Join D to E. Press seam toward E.

7 Join F to DE. Press seam toward F.

8 Join G to DEF. Press seam toward G.

9 Join ABC to DEFG. Press seam toward C.

10 Join H to I. Press seam toward H.

11 Join J to K. Press seam toward J.

12 Join L to JK. Press seam toward JK.

13 Join M to N. Press seam toward M.

14 Join HI to JKL. Press seam toward HI.

15 Join HIJKL to MN. Press seam toward MN.

16 Join ABCDEFG to HIJKLMN. Press seam open.

17 Press block with spray starch.

18 Remove the paper from the back of the block in reverse sewing order for each section.

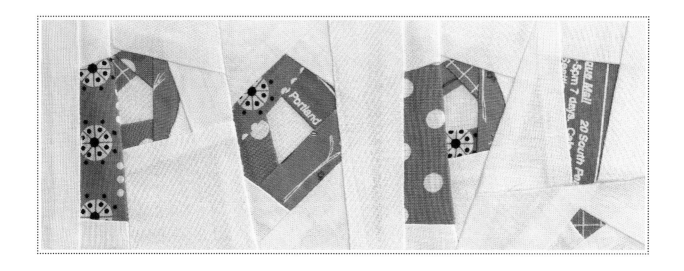

ALLIE-GATOR BABY QUILT

This charming quilt can easily be made for a boy or girl. I think Allie-Gator would be adorable in any fabric you choose, from a pink floral to an orange plaid or a blue polka dot. I hand quilted the project using three strands of embroidery thread, but if you are low on time (or patience!), machine quilt it instead.

featured block
Allie-Gator (page 105)

finished block size
26½" × 16" (67.5 × 40.5 cm)

finished size
36½" × 40½" (92.5 × 103 cm)

Note: This block pattern has been resized for the quilt. Be sure to use the larger project pattern included on the CD when constructing the quilt.

Fabric

- ¼ yd (23 cm) of diagonal plaid print for inside border
- ¾ yd (68.5 cm) of aqua print fabric for outside border
- 1¼ yd (1.2 m) orange polka dot for backing
- 1¼ yd (1.2 m) orange floral fabric for backing
- ⅜ yd (34.5 cm) of black-and-white plaid fabric for binding

For the Allie-Gator block:

- ½ yd (45.5 cm) for background
- One fat quarter for alligator body
- 12" × 4" (30.5 × 10 cm) for spines
- 8" (20.5 cm) square for eye centers and teeth
- 4" (10 cm) square for eye outlines

Other Supplies

- Allie-Gator Baby Quilt block pattern (on CD)
- 40" × 44" (101.5 × 112 cm) piece of batting
- 6-strand embroidery floss (off-white used in the sample) and needle

Tools

- Walking foot (optional)
- Hera marker (optional)

CUT THE FABRIC

From the diagonal plaid print, cut:

- ▶ 2 inner borders, 2¼" × 16½" (5.5 × 42 cm)
- ▶ 2 inner borders, 2¼" × 30½" (5.5 cm × 77.5 cm)

From the aqua print, cut:

- ▶ 2 outer borders, 5½" × 20" (14 × 51 cm)
- ▶ 2 outer borders, 8¾" × 40½" (22 × 103 cm)

From the orange dot, cut on the lengthwise grain:

- ▶ 1 backing rectangle, 44" × 34" (112 × 86.5 cm)

From the orange floral fabric, cut on the lengthwise grain:

- ▶ 1 backing rectangle, 44" × 7" (112 × 18 cm)

From the black-and-white plaid fabric, cut:

- ▶ 4 binding strips, 2½" (6.5 cm) × width of fabric

DIRECTIONS

1 Piece the Allie-Gator Baby Quilt block following the instructions on page 105.

2 Referring to the assembly diagram, sew the two 2¼" × 16½" (5.5 × 42 cm) plaid rectangles to the short ends of the block. Sew the larger plaid rectangles to the top and bottom of the assembled unit. Add the outer border in the same way.

3 Layer the backing, right side down; batting; and quilt top, right side up.

4 Baste the layers together with pins. Mark the quilt top with a diagonal grid of lines 3" (7.5 cm) apart.

5 Hand quilt with a running stitch and three strands of embroidery floss.

6 Use the black-and-white plaid strips to bind the quilt, following the instructions on page 29. Use a walking foot, if desired.

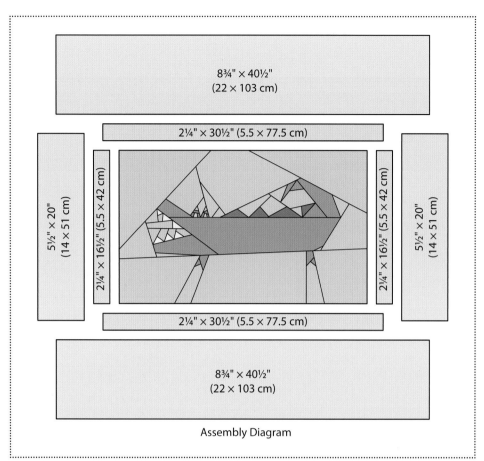

8¾" × 40½"
(22 × 103 cm)

2¼" × 30½" (5.5 × 77.5 cm)

5½" × 20"
(14 × 51 cm)

2¼" × 16½" (5.5 × 42 cm)

2¼" × 16½" (5.5 × 42 cm)

5½" × 20"
(14 × 51 cm)

2¼" × 30½" (5.5 × 77.5 cm)

8¾" × 40½"
(22 × 103 cm)

Assembly Diagram

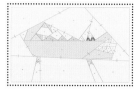

See the CD for the
full-size block pattern.

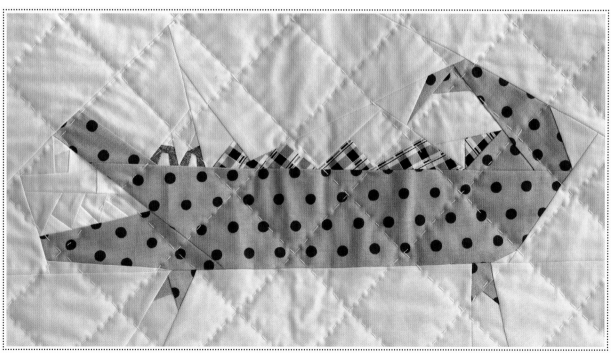

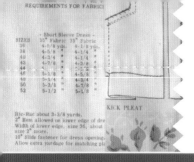

CHAPTER 8

Get Outdoors!

When I'm not sewing, getting outdoors to camp, hike, backpack, ski, or kayak helps to keep my heart happy. These blocks and projects are geared toward getting you out in your backyard for grilling or gardening, or heading to your local park for a picnic.

Block Key

34 BBQ Grill

35 Gardening Hat

36 Picnic Basket

37 Watering Can

38 Seed Packet

39 Watermelon Slice

40 Spade and Hand Rake

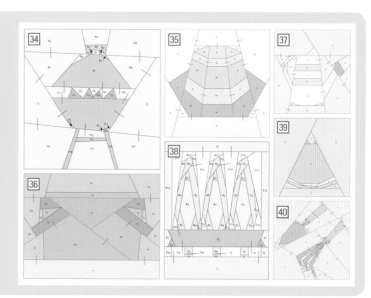

Full-size patterns are included on the CD.

BBQ Grill

Finished Size
6" × 6" (15 × 15 cm)

Fabric Needed
Black-and-white homespun or suiting fabric:
5" (12.5 cm) square for grill body

Brown fabric:
2" (5 cm) square for lid handle

Black print fabric:
4" (10 cm) square for legs and handle supports

Red fabric:
3" (7.5 cm) square for flames

Green-and-white checked fabric:
10" (25.5 cm) square for background

ASSEMBLE THE BLOCK

1 Print the block pattern from the CD onto foundation paper and trim close to the outside edges.

2 Cut the block into sections on the blue lines.

3 Complete all sections, leaving at least ¼" (6 mm) of fabric beyond the edges of each section. Press each section with spray starch. Trim each section ¼" (6 mm) past the pattern edges for the seam allowance.

4 Join C to D. Press seam open.

5 Join B to CD. Press seam toward B.

6 Join E to BCD. Press seam toward E.

7 Join F to BCDE. Press seam toward F.

8 Join G to BCDEF. Press seam toward G.

9 Join A to BCDEFG. Press seam open.

10 Join H to ABCDEFG. Press seam toward H.

11 Press block with spray starch.

12 Remove the paper from the back of the block in reverse sewing order for each section.

Who knew that a grill could have teeth?!
The flames in this grill almost look like teeth, giving the block a whimsical look. The grill block would be perfect for a hot pad or the front of a grilling apron.

Gardening Hat

■ *Let this hat remind you to protect your skin* while you're out gardening, hiking, or relaxing on your deck.

tip
Fussy-cut words or images from the hat accent fabric to feature them in the block; see page 21.

Finished Size
8" × 8" (20.5 × 20.5 cm)

Fabric Needed
Black-and-white windowpane check fabric:
4" (10 cm) square for hat top

White text-print fabric:
5" × 9" (12.5 × 23 cm) for hat accents

Red diagonal plaid print:
6" (15 cm) square for hat body

Red-and-white polka dot fabric:
7" (18 cm) square for brim

Floral print:
10" (25.5 cm) square for background

ASSEMBLE THE BLOCK

1 Print the block pattern from the CD onto foundation paper and trim close to the outside edges.

2 Cut the block into sections on the blue lines.

3 Complete all sections, leaving at least ¼" (6 mm) of fabric beyond the edges of each section. Press each section with spray starch. Trim each section ¼" (6 mm) past the pattern edges for the seam allowance.

4 Join A to B. Press seam open.

5 Join C to AB. Press seam open.

6 Join ABC to D. Press seam open.

7 Join E to ABCD. Press seam open.

8 Join F to ABCDE. Press seam open.

9 Join G to ABCDEF. Press seam open.

10 Press block with spray starch.

11 Remove the paper from the back of the block in reverse sewing order for each section.

Picnic Basket

■ *I imagine this basket filled with* egg salad sandwiches and yummy cakes wrapped in brown glassine bags, tied with kitchen twine. Of course, I'd also have to add my favorite picnic beverage, ginger beer.

Finished Size
8" × 6" (20.5 × 15 cm)

Fabric Needed

Brown-and-white polka dot fabric:
11" (28 cm) square for basket

Woodgrain fabric:
6" (15 cm) square for handles

Red-and-white checked fabric:
3" × 6" (7.5 × 15 cm) for napkin

Black-and-white plaid fabric:
10" × 2" (25.5 × 5 cm) for tablecloth

Green fabric:
10" (25.5 cm) square for background

ASSEMBLE THE BLOCK

❶ Print the block pattern from the CD onto foundation paper and trim close to the outside edges.

❷ Cut the block into sections on the blue lines.

❸ Complete all sections, leaving at least ¼" (6 mm) of fabric beyond the edges of each section. Press each section with spray starch. Trim each section ¼" (6 mm) past the pattern edges for the seam allowance.

❹ Join B to C. Press seam open.

❺ Join A to BC. Press seam toward A.

❻ Join D to E. Press seam open.

❼ Join ABC to DE. Press seam toward ABC.

❽ Join F to ABCDE. Press seam toward F.

❾ Join G to ABCDEF. Press seam open.

❿ Press block with spray starch.

⓫ Remove the paper from the back of the block in reverse sewing order for each section.

Watering Can

■ *This is a great* block for fussy cutting or stamping. Polka dot fabric suggests holes in the spout nozzle.

Finished Size
7½" × 8" (19 × 20.5 cm)

Fabric Needed
White fabric:
7" (18 cm) square for can body

Green word-print fabric:
5" (12.5 cm) square for accents

Black-and-white polka dot fabric:
3" (7.5 cm) for nozzle

Light blue fabric:
One fat eighth for background

ASSEMBLE THE BLOCK

1 Print the block pattern from the CD onto foundation paper and trim close to the outside edges.

2 Cut the block into sections on the blue lines.

3 Complete all sections, leaving at least ¼" (6 mm) of fabric beyond the edges of each section. Press each section with spray starch. Trim each section ¼" (6 mm) past the pattern edges for the seam allowance.

4 Join A to D. Press seam open.

5. Join B to C. Press seam open.

6 Join AD to BC. Press seam open.

7 Join ABCD to E. Press seam open.

8 Press block with spray starch.

9 Remove the paper from the back of the block in reverse sewing order for each section.

Seed Packet

Finished Size
4½" × 5¾" (11.5 × 14.5 cm)

Fabric Needed
White fabric:
7" (18 cm) square for background

Light blue fabric:
2" × 6" (5 × 15 cm) for label

Green print fabric:
7" (18 cm) square for corn husks

Yellow print fabric:
5" (12.5 cm) square for corn kernel

Dark green fabric:
2" (5 cm) square for corn detail

Pink polka dot fabric:
7" (18 cm) square for border

Other Supplies
Letter stamps
Permanent fabric ink

ASSEMBLE THE BLOCK

1 Print the block pattern from the CD onto foundation paper and trim close to the outside edges.

2 Cut the block into sections on the blue lines.

3 Following the stamping instructions on page 26, stamp "sweet corn" on the label fabric.

4 Complete all sections, leaving at least ¼" (6 mm) of fabric beyond the edges of each section. Press each section with spray starch. Trim each section ¼" (6 mm) past the pattern edges for the seam allowance.

5 Join A to B. Press seam open.

6 Join C to AB. Press open.

7 Join D to ABC. Press toward D.

8 Join E to F. Press seam open.

Seed packets are so inspiring to me, with all their tiny detail. How about making a little oilcloth-lined snack pouch with this cutie for decoration?

9 Join G to H. Press seam toward H.

10 Join I to GH. Press seam toward GH.

11 Join J to GHI. Press seam toward J.

12 Join ABCD to EF. Press seam toward EF.

13 Join ABCDEF to GHIJ. Press seam open.

14 Press block with spray starch.

15 Remove the paper from the back of the block in reverse sewing order for each section.

Watermelon Slice

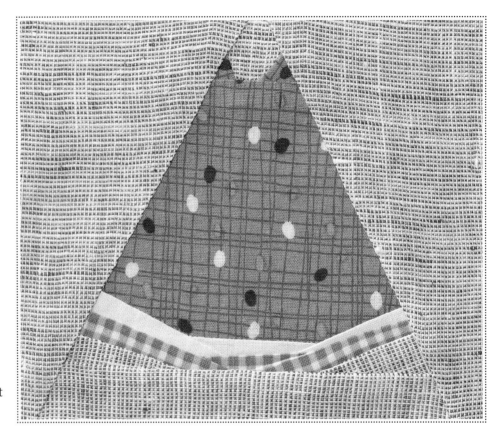

■ *To make the watermelon slice* realistic, use a fabric with light and dark spots for the watermelon flesh. This block would be perfect to perk up a set of outdoor place mats.

Finished Size
6" × 6" (15 × 15 cm)

Fabric Needed

Pink print fabric:
6" (15 cm) square for watermelon

White fabric:
4" (10 cm) square for inner rind

Green-and-white checked fabric:
4" (10 cm) square for outer rind

Blue-and-white homespun or linen fabric:
10" (25.5 cm) square for background

ASSEMBLE THE BLOCK

1 Print the block pattern from the CD onto foundation paper and trim close to the outside edges.

2 There is only one section in this block. Paper piece the block, leaving at least ¼" (6 mm) of fabric beyond the edges of the pattern. Trim ¼" (6 mm) past the pattern edges for the seam allowance.

3 Press the block with starch.

4 Remove paper from the back of the block in reverse sewing order.

Spade and Hand Rake

Finished Size
9" × 9" (23 × 23 cm)

Fabric Needed
Brown-and-beige homespun or linen fabric:
10" (25.5 cm) square for handles

Black text-print fabric:
10" (25.5 cm) square for tools

Pink floral fabric:
One fat quarter for background

ASSEMBLE THE BLOCK

① Print the block pattern from the CD onto foundation paper and trim close to the outside edges.

② Cut the block into sections on the blue lines.

③ Complete all sections, leaving at least ¼" (6 mm) of fabric beyond the edges of each section. Press each section with spray starch. Trim each section ¼" (6 mm) past the pattern edges for the seam allowance.

④ Join A to B. Press seam open.

⑤ Join C to AB. Press seam open.

⑥ Join D to ABC. Press seam open.

⑦ Join E to ABCD. Press toward E.

⑧ Join F to ABCDE. Press seam open.

⑨ Join G to ABCDEF. Press seam toward G.

⑩ Join H to I. Press seam toward I.

⑪ Join J to HI. Press seam toward J.

⑫ Join K to HIJ. Press seam toward K.

⑬ Join L to M. Press seam toward M.

⑭ Join N to LM. Press seam toward N.

⑮ Join O to LMN. Press seam toward O.

⑯ Join P to Q. Press seam toward Q.

⑰ Join HIJK to LMNO. Press seam toward HIJK.

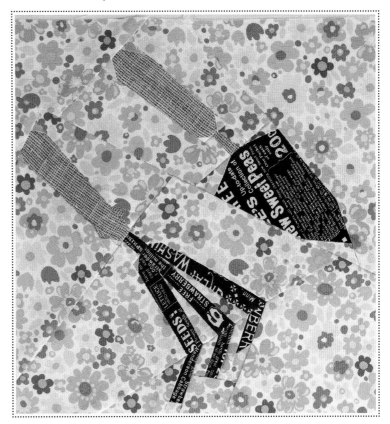

■ *A spade and hand rake are perfect for your* flower garden exploits. A knee cushion with weatherproof or oilcloth fabric on the back and this block, enlarged or bordered, on the front could be so charming. Your knees will thank you!

⑱ Join PQ to HIJKLMNO. Press seam toward LMNO.

⑲ Join ABCDEFG to HIJKLMNOPQ. Press seam open.

⑳ Press block with spray starch.

㉑ Remove the paper from the back of the block in reverse sewing order for each section.

GARDENING APRON

With its clever construction, this gardening apron is just the right size to keep your gardening tools at hand. Substitute a small hand rake or spade (or both) from the Spade and Hand Rake block (page 125) for the Seed Packet, or maybe a Watering Can block (page 122) is more your style?

featured block
Seed Packet (page 123)

finished block size
3⅜" × 4⅜" (8.6 × 11 cm)

finished size
20¼" × 12½" (51.5 × 31.5 cm), excluding ties

Note: This block pattern has been resized for the apron. Be sure to use the smaller project pattern on the CD when constructing the apron.

Fabric Needed

- Fabrics for Seed Packet block on page 123; choose a micro-dot print for the border and a text print for the label
- ½ yd (45.5 cm) of red-and-white polka dot home décor fabric for apron front
- ½ yd (45.5 cm) of multicolored print quilting cotton apron backing
- ¼ yd (23 cm) of off-white canvas for pocket lining
- One fat eighth of brown-and-beige print quilting cotton for pocket
- ¼ yd (23 cm) blue-and-white striped fabric for waistband and ties

Other Supplies

Printed apron, pocket, and Seed Packet Apron block patterns (on CD)

Tools

- Size 50 binding tape maker (optional)
- Chalk marker (I use a Clover Chaco Liner)

CUT THE FABRIC

From the red-and-white polka dot home décor fabric, cut:

▶ 1 apron, using the apron pattern (on CD)

From the multicolored print quilting cotton, cut:

▶ 1 apron lining, using the apron pattern (on CD)

From the off-white canvas, cut:

▶ 1 pocket lining, using the apron pocket pattern (on CD)

From the brown-and-beige print quilting cotton, cut:

▶ 2 center panels, 3⅞" × 2" (9.8 × 5 cm)

▶ 2 side panels, 7½" × 7 ⅞" (19 × 20 cm)

From the blue-and-white striped fabric, cut:

▶ 2 waistband/tie strips, 3½" (9 cm) × width of fabric

tip

If you're not a gardener, try making this apron with a kitchen- or craft-themed block on the pocket.

DIRECTIONS

1 Make one Seed Packet apron block from the pattern on the CD, following the instructions on page 123.

2 Sew the center panels to the top and bottom edges of the Seed Packet block.

3 Sew the side panels to the sides of the assembled unit.

4 Fold the assembled pocket strip in half from top to bottom, centering the fold on the Seed Packet block. Pin the pocket pattern to the assembled pocket strip, aligning the fold line with the fabric fold, and cut out the pocket.

5 With right sides together, pin the bottom of the apron backing to the lower edge of the pocket and sew. Repeat to stitch the apron front to the pocket lining's lower edge.

6 With right sides together, pin the assembled units together and sew, leaving the top edge open.

7 Trim the corners diagonally to reduce bulk and clip the seam allowances along the curves. Turn the apron right side out and press.

8 Edgestitch the apron's side edges from the upper edge to the pocket seam. Stitch again ¼" (6 mm) inside the first stitches.

9 Edgestitch the upper edge of the pocket. Stitch again, ¼" (6 mm) from the first stitches.

10 Fold the pocket to the front side of the apron along the apron-to-pocket seam. Pin the pocket sides in place. Edgestitch the sides of the pocket from the pocket upper edge to the lower edge of the pocket and apron. Stitch again ¼" (6 mm) from the first stitches.

11 Use chalk to mark the top edge of the pocket 4½" (11.5 cm) from each side. Mark the bottom edge of the pocket 5" (12.5 cm) from each side. Align a ruler with the marks on the left side and draw a chalk line connecting the marks. Repeat to connect the lines on the right.

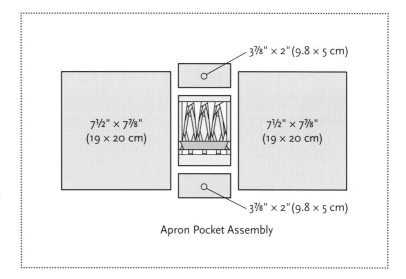

3⅞" × 2" (9.8 × 5 cm)

7½" × 7⅞"
(19 × 20 cm)

7½" × 7⅞"
(19 × 20 cm)

3⅞" × 2" (9.8 × 5 cm)

Apron Pocket Assembly

12 Topstitch ⅛" (3 mm) from both sides of each chalk line, creating a double line of topstitching at each location and dividing the pocket into three sections.

13 Remove the selvages and sew the two waistband/ties together to make a long strip. Press the seam open. Trim the strip to 60" (152.5 cm).

14 Press ½" (1.3 cm) to the wrong side along each long edge of the strip. Fold the strip in half lengthwise, wrong sides together, and press again. Optionally, use a size 50 bias tape maker to prepare the strip.

15 Unfold the ends of the binding and press ¼" (6 mm) to the wrong side on each end. Refold and press again.

16 Center the binding along the top edge of the apron. Slide the apron between the binding folds so that the binding encloses the apron's raw edge.

17 Topstitch ⅛" (3 mm) from all four edges of the binding, aligning the folded edges of each tie as you sew.

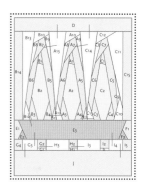

See the CD for the full-size block pattern.

Resources

FABRIC AND SEWING SUPPLIES

Amazon
amazon.com
VersaCraft ink pads; freezer paper sheets

B-Right-On Sewing Center
965 Platte River Blvd., Unit S
Brighton, CO 80601
(720) 685-3392
Sewing machine and fabric

C. Jenkins Company
39 S. Schlueter Ave.
Dellwood, MO 63135
cjenkinscompany.com
Bubble Jet Set products

Connecting Threads
13118 NE 4th St.
Vancouver, WA 98684
(360) 260-8900
connectingthreads.com
Fons and Porter glue stick

Fabric.com
(888) 455-2940
fabric.com
Fabric

Fabrics-store.com
(866) 620-2008
fabrics-store.com
Linen fabrics

Fat Quarter Shop
PO Box 1544
Manchaca, TX 78652
(866) 826-2069
Email kimberly@fatquartershop.com
fatquartershop.com
Fabric

Joann Fabric and Craft Stores
(888) 739-4120
joann.com
VersaCraft ink pads; Insul-Bright batting; Clover fork pins

Just Curves
PO Box 591
Hunt, TX 78024-0591
(830) 238-7605
Email: justcurves@earthlink.net
justcurves.biz
Seam roller

Lee Valley Tools Ltd.
PO Box 6295, Station J
Ottawa, ON K2A 1T4
CANADA
(800) 267-8767 (to place an order)
(800) 267-8761 (customer service)
leevalley.com
Seam ripper

Mama Said Sew
406 N. College Ave.
Fort Collins, CO 80524
(970) 493-0623
mamasaidsew.com
Fabric

Marmalade Fabrics
marmaladefabrics.com
Fabric

Pink Castle Fabrics
3808 Plaza Dr., Ste. A
Ann Arbor, MI 48108
(877) 808-8695
pinkcastlefabrics.com
Fabric

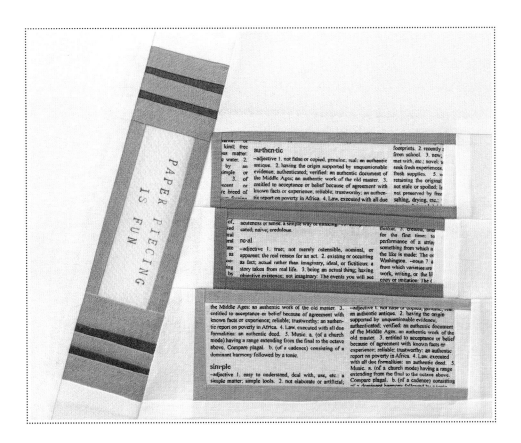

Saral Paper Corp.
400 E. 55th St., Ste. 18B
New York, NY 10022
saralpaper.com/main.html
Saral transfer paper

Spoonflower, Inc.
2810 Meridian Pkwy., Ste. 176
Durham, NC 27713
(919) 886-7885
spoonflower.com
Specialty print fabrics

Superbuzzy
superbuzzy.com/shop
Karisma glue stick and Japanese fabric

RECOMMENDED READING LIST

Koseki, Suzuko. *Natural Patchwork: 26 Stylish Projects Inspired by Flowers, Fabric, and Home.* Boston, Massachusetts: Roost Books, 2011.

Koseki, Suzuko. *Patchwork Style: 35 Simple Projects for a Cozy and Colorful Life.* Boston, Massachusetts: Roost Books, 2009.

Koseki, Suzuko. *Playful Patchwork.* Minneapolis, Minnesota: Creative Publishing Lifestyle, 2011.

McDowell, Ruth. *Ruth B. McDowell's Piecing Workshop.* Concord, California: C&T Publishing, 2007.

Sew-Ichigo at sew-ichigo.blogspot.com

Takahashi, Ayumi. *Patchwork Please!: Colorful Zakka Projects to Stitch and Give.* Fort Collins, Colorado: Interweave, 2013.

Selected Templates

Café
Pâtisserie

Embroidery Diagram for Café Pâtisserie Curtain (page 40).
Copy at 100%.

seam ripper

markers

ruler

rotary
cutters

scissors

Embroidery Diagram for Sewing Organizer (page 100).
Copy at 100%.

Index

Find fresh, colorful projects and inspiration

with these resources from Interweave

PATCHWORK, PLEASE!
Colorful Zakka Projects
to Stitch and Give
Ayumi Takahashi
ISBN 978-1-59668-599-4, $22.95

I LOVE PATCHWORK
21 Irresistible Zakka
Projects to Sew
Rashida Coleman-Hale
ISBN 978-1-59668-142-2, $24.95

**THE QUILTER'S
APPLIQUÉ WORKSHOP**
Timeless Techniques for
Modern Designs
Kevin Kosbab
ISBN 978-1-59668-861-2, $26.99

Available at your favorite retailer or **sew**daily shop shop.sewdaily.com

sewdaily | sewing made modern.

Stitch magazine is all about creating with fabric and thread. Offering a fresh perspective on sewing, it's loaded with clever projects and modern designs. Find trendy and classic projects with step-by-step instructions, chats with inspiring designers, and the latest in sewing notions, fabrics, and patterns.
Interweavestitch.com

Sew Daily is the ultimate online community for sewing enthusiasts. Get e-newsletters, download free articles and eBooks, discover tips and tricks from the experts, and find general all-around sewing information! Sign up at **SewDaily.com.**